SCIENCE IN THE
ELEMENTARY SCHOOL

A Worktext

Harold R. Hungerford

Audrey N. Tomera

Science Education Center
Dept. of Curr., Instr., & Media
Southern Illinois University
Carbondale, Illinois 62901

ISBN 0-87563-132-0

Published by
STIPES PUBLISHING COMPANY
10 - 12 Chester Street
Champaign, Illinois 61820

jwc   8/6/79

ACKNOWLEDGEMENTS

It is entirely fitting that numerous persons and agencies be given credit in the production of this worktext, whether said credit reflects assistance in the past or in the present. Many have been the methods students who, over the years, have suffered through our efforts to design for them the best, well-rounded methods course possible. Student reaction to the materials have done much to improve the readings and activities included here.

Similarly, as the handouts thrust themselves from both ditto and mimeograph machine, a good many people were willing to give editorial opinions concerning same. Included would be Ron and Linda Gardella, Ralph Litherland, Roger Robinson, David Miles, Gary Harvey, Morris Lamb, and Kevin Swick. Also involved in subsequent editorial work were Peter Rubba, Donna Childers, and Pat Patinella, all of whom contributed a great deal to the final product. In addition, the authors would like to express their thanks to the Commission on Science Education of the AAAS for its willingness to permit the writers to quote directly materials from the SAPA program.

And then there were those who, believing in the authors, willingly taught the original editions of what is found in this worktext. Henry Walding, Bill Bluhm, Ron Gardella, and Bahman Saghatchian draw praise for their dynamic, compassionate, and competent teaching!

Publishing deadlines always seem a bit ethereal and traumatic at best. Yet, in the case of this worktext, it was met with time to spare. Meeting this deadline was not totally a function of the compulsive nature of the authors. A tremendous amount of time was devoted to manuscript preparation and art work by both Bill Bluhm and Henry Frazier. The authors could not have been on time without their contributions and selfless support. In addition, R. Ben Peyton is responsible for a great deal of productive creativity with respect to the environmental education section of this publication. The authors have included liberal portions of his early work in this important area.

Harold R. Hungerford
Audrey N. Tomera

TABLE OF CONTENTS

PART I

On Understanding Science and Technology

Performance Objectives

Subsequent to your interaction with Part I you will be expected to be able to . . .

1. . . . explain why science was created by man and why it must be considered as a product of man's intellect.

2. . . . define, or identify an accurate definition of empiricism.

3. . . . defend the position that science has but one ethic - the ethic of empiricism.

4. . . . describe the characteristic(s) of scientific truth that separate science from other kinds of truth bases, e.g., authority, faith, religious dogma.

5. . . . define, or identify accurate definitions of process and product as associated with science.

6. . . . describe and/or diagram the relationship that exists between process and product and explain why this relationship is considered to be a cyclical one.

7. . . . differentiate between science and technology.

8. . . . based upon your answer to objective 7 above, identify two (2) misconceptions that humans have concerning science and technology.

9. . . . defend the idea that science and technology must be separated conceptually in the minds of both teachers and students.

> . . . every citizen (must) have a basic and functional understanding of the products of science - the concepts, the principles and the facts; and be able to understand and use the process of science - the modes of thought, the attitudes of mind, the tactics and strategy, and the appreciations, . . . This goal can be achieved through the schools . . . It must have the support of every citizen in every local community. It will require a concerted and organized effort, but these costs are low when weighed against the realization that this kind of education in science may be basic to our survival.
>
> Ellsworth S. Obourn - 1961

1

On Understanding Science and Technology

Science in itself furnishes none of the ends of action;
in so far as the knowledge of the scientist is concerned,
it is immaterial whether what we know of high explosives
is used to build a great reservoir to make the desert
blossom as the rose, or to construct giant shells to
snuff out the lives of an entire city. As a man the
scientist may, nay, must, make some preference; but the
grounds for that preference are not to be found in physics.

Columbia Associates in
Philosophy - 1923

Philosophers and common men alike have struggled over the centuries in
an attempt to perceive man's true role in the universe as well as his
destiny. Unfortunately, we look at man and find him almost unbearably
complex and mostly uninterpreted. Man, unlike the other creatures to whom
he is related anatomically and physiologically, is blessed - or burdened
perhaps - with a highly developed, curiosity-oriented brain. The complexity
of this organ does not permit him to escape the inexorable ties to the
biosphere which he shares with other animate creatures but it does permit
him what many would call the rationality and responsibility of being human.
This, of course, refers to man's ability to look at his environment, interpret it, and solve those tangible problems with which he chooses to cope.

This rational quality of man separates him from the rest of the living
creatures on the earth. It allows him to develop the thing called culture
and all of the blessings and problems that culture brings with it. One of
the products of man's mind, and an integral part of his culture, is science!

The writers who have dealt with the question, "What is science?" are
many. If there exist numerous responses to this question then why do we
contend with it here? The answer is simple. Those who propose to guide
students' minds toward accurate concepts concerning science and scientists,
(and this includes you) must have clear and thorough concepts themselves
before they can adequately broach the topic in the classroom. Indeed, the
lack of accurate concepts of science and scientists may well provide a
partial answer to help explain a lack of understanding concerning what
science education should encompass. It seems to the writers that prime prerequisites for competent science instruction (and learning) are workable and
accurate concepts of science and the scientist.

What Is
Science?   This question, given to any large population of rational human beings, produces a
wide array of responses. Perhaps the most
aesthetic and least meaningful definition is to say that science is inquiry.
This pleases almost everyone but it fails to communicate what science is
because there is usually a wide spectrum of interpretation regarding "inquiry".

Man is, to a great extent, a curious animal. One has only to observe children discovering new things or listen to the gossip in the beauty shop to find evidence of this. Similarly, man's tremendous intellect finds an uneasy peace when something exists within his limits of perception and remains uninterpreted. His almost insatiable drive to "understand" in order to satisfy his curiosity had caused the creation of the cultural enterprise called science.

Man searches for truth in many dimensions. However, only one kind of truth is accepted by the men who are called scientists. This ethic of science, or truth base, is called empiricism. In essence this form of truth (empircism) is based on the belief that only those factors which man can experience directly or indirectly through his senses have reality. Empiricism differs from a reality base of faith or belief in authority. It is this quality that separates science from authority based truth or dogma, e.g., religious faith.

Sensory reality or experimental truth - often called empiricism - brings into being that dimension of man's culture called science! (Note: Empiricism is often referred to as the generation of knowledge about something by experimental means or direct observation. It involves data produced through scientific process - data which are replicable by other members of the scientific community). Stated in a simpler manner, we might say that science is man's way of investigating the objects and events of the total environment in a manner that provides empirical knowledge of these objects and events.

Science differs from metaphysical or ethical knowledge in that scientific knowledge is empirically truthful or at least supported by empirical evidence. There is little room for faith alone or intuition in science. Regardless of the value of a scientist's intuitive judgment, his intuition must eventually be replaced by an empirical construct or his investigation is worthless. Man has demanded this of science and, as a consequence, science has little else to offer! Science is a human enterprise constructed on one ethic and one alone - that of empiricism.

This ethic has often caused problems for the scientific enterprise for science ends with the creation of empirical data. Science assumes no other moral or ethical responsibility. It is what man himself does with empirical data that leads to moral dilemmas. This is one of the most difficult concepts for students to assimilate . . . that moral judgments are not in the realm of the working scientists - only empirical judgments count when science is being conducted.

The Process and Product of Science

The means by which science investigates the universe are many. The old shopworn slogan for the tool of science is the "scientific method". This is a grave error. To limit science to one, highly-structured investigation strategy is to absurdly oversimplify the entire endeavor. Science is a wide array of intellectual scientific processes whereby man can generate or discover data. The simplest, yet one of the most productive, is observation. The most complex is experimentation. Other scientific processes used are classification, inferring, controlling variables, hypothesizing, measuring and so on. Although all intellectual science processes are not mentioned here, it is hoped that the reader will realize that the processes are many and varied - not <u>one</u> in nature. They are a reservoir of mental skills that can be called on by scientists when needed. These intellectual skills constitute the process aspect of science - the means of empiricism - the means by which men generate knowledge concerning the environment about them.

As lucid as the notion of process may appear to the reader it is only part of the story of science. Process may be the means but what of the end? The end, of course, is knowledge or <u>product</u>. Product is, in science, the purpose of process. Without the vast reservoir of knowledge science has contributed, process would be totally inconclusive and the enterprise of science a mute issue.

Thus we can see that science is a combination of two things - process and product. The relationship between the two, however, is seldom directional. Process breeds product but with new knowledge usually comes more questions that impose new demands on process. Similarly, scientific product is always amenable to modification as the result of continuing scientific inquiry. It is unlikely that the cyclical nature of process and product would ever end in a healthy cultural setting.

SCIENCE

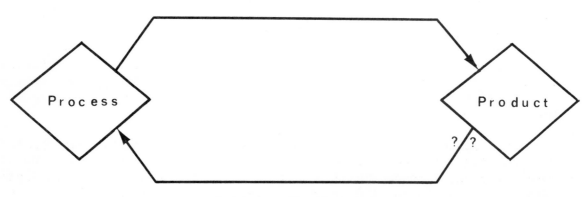

Ethic : Empiricism

And What of Technology?

The distinction between science and technology is an important dichotomy with several implications for education. How man uses the knowledge of science (use = technology) constitutes a distinct and separate cultural component from science per se.

Technology is simply "applied science". In our discussion of technology we will arbitrarily refer to the term as meaning <u>any socio-cultural application of scientific product</u>. Fleming's scientific discovery of penicillin, when used to treat strep throat or gonorrhea, becomes a medical-technological

application. It is no longer scientific product. The brilliant investigations of Oersted and Faraday on the relationships between electricity
and magnetism, done early in the Nineteenth Century, were pure scientific
research. Neither man would have dreamed of the technological applications
made of their research in telephone and telegraph communications alone.
The knowledge about penicillin's antibiotic power or the relationship between electricity and magnetism is scientific - the application or socio-
cultural use is technological.

Implications of the
Science - Technological
Dichotomy -

Because of the public nature of the
knowledge of science, it becomes an
entity whose use is utterly dependent

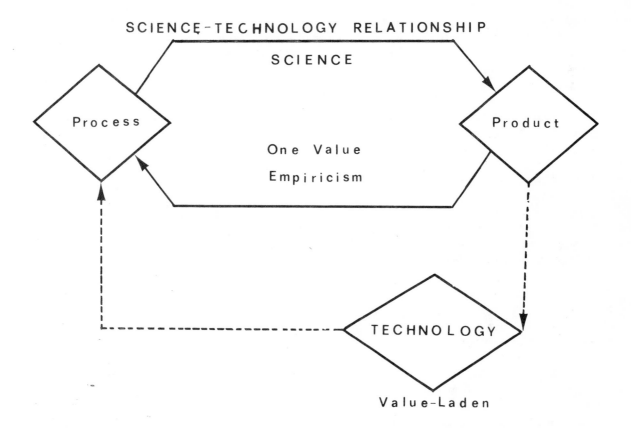

SCIENCE-TECHNOLOGY RELATIONSHIP

SCIENCE

Process

One Value

Empiricism

Product

TECHNOLOGY

Value-Laden

on the whim and moral discretions (or indiscretions) of anyone or any group
intelligent enough to make use of that knowledge. Science cannot and should
not bear the responsibility for technological tragedy or triumph. Society
uses both science and technology for its own purposes - good or bad. Man
himself must claim credit for the outcomes of his technological uses of
scientific information. Human beings, not science or technology, must assume
responsibility for their own destiny based on their own value-ridden decisions.
The scientist as a scientist has little control over how society chooses to
use the products of science. He operates only within the ethic of empiricism.
There are those who would like to place immense responsibility as to how

knowledge is used on the scientific community. To do so is to fail to understand the empirical base of the discipline itself. The scientist can often sway public opinion with his immense knowledge but he does <u>not</u> control society any more than any other intelligent person.

One of the most classic cases is probably the intriguing story of Alfred Nobel, the chemist who developed dynamite in 1867. This development, in Nobel's mind, would be a useful instrument for social good. But, social destruction substituted for much of Nobel's naive desire. Death and destruction were partners with the political decisions to use dynamite for war. Nobel hated this but had no control over the ways society chose to use dynamite. As a consequence of his guilt-ridden conscience, Nobel set aside some $9,000,000 in an interest-bearing fund. The interest from this fund goes to award the annual Nobel prizes for peace, medicine, and many other fields. The point here is simply Nobel's complete inability to control his own discovery. To say that any scientist or technologist must bear total responsibility for the cultural applications of his finding is as absurd as trying to bring Orville and Wilbur Wright back from their graves to stand trial for the failure of Apollo 13.

The answers to man's most perplexing problems lie not in science or in the irrational ethical demands placed on scientists - the answers lie in the ways in which knowledge is used and the manner in which humans behave. These are socio-political and technological considerations for the most part and not scientific ones! Every member of society should realize that science is solely an empirical, intellectual act of man. Science in nothing more than the <u>processes</u> man uses to generate scientific knowledge and the <u>product</u> or scientific information generated. Science cannot solve problems; it can only provide the information for man to choose to use. Just as science bears no blame for causing man's problems, it also accepts no responsibility for solving man's problem situations. Humans cause their own problems; it is up to them, not science, to find successful solutions to the problems they have created. It is imperative for children (and adults) to conceptualize science and technology in this manner as well as to correctly perceive its potential and its limitations.

Implications For
Elementary Teachers -
The above discussion in terms of the differences between science and technology and the varying ethics of each may alone be the most single important idea about science generated in this methods book. If teachers of science have clear concepts of science and technology, they, in turn, can transmit these concepts accurately to their students. Teachers can then plan for a science program that accurately reflects the essence of science. Teachers will have the ability to point out where technological applications of science have been made and how they relate to the scientific enterprise. You, as elementary teachers, have the unique opportunity to clarify your own thinking and influence the understanding of your students.

PART II

Why Science Instruction for Children?

Performance Objectives

Subsequent to your interactions with Part II, you will be expected to be able to . . .

1. . . . define the term "general education" as well as list and describe the characteristics which typify a general education for all children.

2. . . . identify and/or list the components of "scientific literacy" as stated by the authors of the worktext. Further, you will be expected to be able to list or identify the elements found within each component, e.g., be able to list at least eight scientific processes associated with the process category of literacy.

3. . . . communicate a rationale for using "scientific literacy" as a basic argument for teaching science to children.

4. . . . communicate a rationale for the various elements which are described under each category of scientific literacy. Said rationale should include, in part, those dividends cited for students as a consequence of becoming scientifically literate.

5. . . . write a paragraph which clearly demonstrates that you understand the relationships which exist between those literacy dividends described for students and the components of scientific literacy as identified in Part II of the worktext.

6. . . . list and/or describe the values to be found in science education from the teacher's perspective, e.g., using science as a content vehicle in the language arts. Further, you will be expected to be able to argue the educational significance of these values.

Why Science Instruction for Children?

In the opinion of the writers, the only sound argument for educating children is that of providing them with a sound "general education". A general education is one which provides human beings with the knowledge and skills which will enable them to be effective and well-adjusted members of society both today and tomorrow. This strongly infers that there must be some very generic or generalized bodies of knowledge and skills which are pertinent in the lives of all human beings. It also infers that the elementary school should probably not be an institution for specializing and segregating children academically in order to reach different goals for different groups. The entire premise of "general education" is one based on the notion that a commonality of preparation for life is of paramount importance and that the components of this curriculum can be identified and operationally defined.

It follows that all major instructional areas existing in today's elementary schools are considered of value by society for general education purposes. Whether or not this is the case, one can observe that science is finding an ever increasing role in the nation's schools and, therefore, science must be considered as an integral component in a child's general education.

However, science instruction is by no means consistent across the schools of America. Nor can we always observe science being taught. There are times when the preservice teacher - and, indeed, oftentimes the inservice teacher - finds it difficult to provide a sound argument for science instruction. In fact, science often takes a "back seat" to other curricular areas and does so for a wide variety of reasons. These reasons include the "back to basics" argument so often heard today, the "lack of time for science" position, the teacher's feeling of insecurity with science, or simply a lack of motivation on the part of the teacher to provide experientially-based science instruction. The writers believe that most of the reasons for ignoring science or arguing its value are faulty and stem from a basic lack of understanding of what science is, its role in man's society, and its impact (and potential impact) on children.

Part II of your worktext, therefore, is designed to discuss science from a general education perspective and to help eliminate the faulty educational perspectives concerning science so often observed in both pre and inservice teachers. Because of this, the writers ask that you carefully consider the positions which follow and the logic behind these positions. Of paramount importance is your own professional responsibility to clarify your own understanding of science and its role in a general education. Only by achieving such clarification can you teach science in order to maximize its potential for elementary school children both today and tomorrow.

Scientific Literacy –
The Major Consideration

Science has had and is having a tremendous impact on man and his culture. Whether we like it or not, we must be able to cope each and every day in an environment that is science and technologically oriented. This fact alone is probably a sufficient argument for placing an emphasis on science in the elementary school. As meaningful as this argument may be, the writers believe that there are many other reasons for incorporating science in the curriculum. However, all of these reasons may be discussed under one overall heading. This heading is commonly termed "scientific literacy". Of course, "literacy" in this context goes beyond the constraints normally placed on a definition of literacy. It is more than being able to read and write about science.

In the field of science education there is some disagreement as to what constitutes "scientific literacy". Still, there are some common elements that the writers believe to be critical to a child's general education. These are the elements that will be presented here and the ones we expect you to conceptualize and be able to implement in your own classroom.

The Elements of
Literacy –

What follows is an effort to list and describe the various elements of scientific literacy. As you read these elements and the discussion associated with each you should likewise grow to understand the necessity for incorporating these elements into your instructional program in science.

A scientifically literate human being can be described as one who . . . (1) . . . has a correct concept of what science is and what it is not. As noted earlier, science is simply a special way of investigating the objects and events of the universe. It is based on a philosophy of what is reality and this philosophy dictates some rules that must be respected when man searches for scientific knowledge. A critical basis of science is its empirical nature. Empiricism is observation or experimentation oriented. And, similarly, knowledge can be empirical only if it can be replicated. This means simply that the observation or the experiment can be repeated and shown valid. Scientists also believe that man must consider knowledge to be tentative. The scientist perceives that knowledge is subject to change. Interestingly, children (and some adults too) believe that scientific knowledge as an absolute truth value. This is not the case at all! Most scientific knowledge is inductively derived knowledge and subject to change as a result of new observations. Much of what scientists "know" is constantly being modified as a function of new information.

In addition, scientific knowledge is usually perceived as being probabilistic. Here, again, we see a characteristic closely allied to the tentative nature of knowledge in science. Much of what we derive from research is a function of probabilities. A tremendous amount of the knowledge in the behavioral sciences (e.g., psychology) is a function of probabilities rather than absolute, dogmatic conclusions. How often do you hear something like, "One who is male and smokes two packs of cigarettes a day will have a greater probability of respiratory disease than . . ." This statement is based on probabilities rather than on certainties. This is what science is all about. It permits man to predict future happenings with a high level of confidence.

And, finally, scientists believe that scientific knowledge should be public. This is an ethic which is sometimes violated by the scientific community but one which is a basic belief nevertheless. Probably the most prevalent reason for arguing for public knowledge is one closely associated with replicability. If knowledge is made public, its "goodness" or veracity can be tested by other scientists under similar conditions.

(2) . . . understands the relationships which exist between science and technology and how these pursuits influence society. Among other things, children should understand that there are striking differences between science and technology. At the same time, the child should understand that science and technology tend to support each other and that the relationship between the two is a close one. This is rather like looking at both sides of the coin, and it is imperative that this be accomplished.

Allied with the above, the writers firmly believe that citizens (young and old alike) must realize the tremendous limitations of science and technology. Far too many people tend to see science and technology as omnipotent or all-powerful although this is totally absurd. This perception tends to permit citizens to foolishly rely on science and technology to solve many of the persistent problems facing man. In reality, science and technology are man-controlled and capable of solving only those problems which are amenable to investigation and solution by technological means. Most of man's problems must be faced squarely by man acting in consort with other human beings in a citizenship capacity and not by relying on either science or technology. It appears cogent to help youngsters perceive that they cannot abdicate their own responsibilities to science and technology.

Further, it is important for human beings to realize that the activities of science and technology are controlled by society. Society has certain perceived needs and these are often translated into demands on science and technology. These demands can be humanistically oriented, politically oriented, or economically oriented or combinations of these. Of course, a good deal of what science researches is science-oriented - science for its own sake so to speak - the search for knowledge as a function of man's curiosity. This basic curiosity has led to some of the most startling discoveries ever made. Consider the X-ray, the research leading to the theory of evolution, space exploration, etc., etc.

Closely associated with the above characteristic of science is another that deals with the value of scientific knowledge. Oftentimes what science discovers is seemingly with little merit as far as technology or society is concerned. However, time after time, seemingly valueless knowledge has turned out to be of considerable importance later on. Many, for example, believe that the nation's space program is a waste of money. Another decade or tens of decades may prove that the expenditure of money was very efficient indeed. What breakthroughs are ahead in harnessing the vast amounts of energy

that exist throughout the universe? Could the seemingly silly research
on solar winds provide man with a basically free transportation energy
source down the road? Are the natural resources of the moon and Mars
possible resources for man on earth in another twenty years? Can what we
have learned about man's physical reactions in space be converted to save
lives on earth? On and on . . . The vast backlog of scientific knowledge
being gained in a multitude of research studies can have tremendous consequences for man's own survival in the future.

(3) . . . understands and can apply key concepts of scientific
knowledge in his daily life. Knowledge, in part, permits man to acquire
new knowledge. This, of course, is done via the process-product cycle
with which you are already familiar. Knowledge also helps free man from
the chains of superstition. Although there is no complete agreement as to
what constitutes this literacy component, it is obvious that certain key
concepts are of great importance in a sound general education. A few of
these concepts which the writers and others perceive to be important follow
for purposes of example.

The idea that things happen in the universe because of cause and effect
relationships appears critical. The cause and effect concept has a close
relationship to understanding that the universe is more or less orderly and
that happenings can be predicted with high degrees of probability. Naturally,
this idea should also have the impact of allaying many of man's superstitions.

Concepts dealing with the relationships between matter and energy also
appear critical to literacy. Human beings interact with these relationships
each and every day of their lives. What are the relationships? Can matter
and energy be universally conserved? Are there exceptions to this conservation? What are the implications of these ideas to human beings as they
interact with the environment?

The concept of homeostasis should probably be considered as a key
concept in the literacy dimension. Homeostasis can be defined as a state
of equilibrium or a tendency toward such a state between different but
interdependent elements. On the surface, this appears to be quite an idea -
too difficult, perhaps, for children. Not true! A healthy organism is
homeostatic. The bits and pieces of that organism are working together
successfully - in equilibrium if you will. More importantly for children,
perhaps, is the notion of homeostasis as it involves their environment.
Are living communities becoming less and less balanced as a function of man's
activities? Or, are they able to sustain homeostasis? Is man in a
homeostatic relationship with the biosphere or are there severe threats to
this equilibrium? The ecological implications of homeostasis are significant
and of importance to every man, woman, and child on the planet earth.

Concepts concerning both asexual and sexual reproduction seem appropriate
for a list of key concepts. All living species must be able to reproduce
themselves or become extinct. Further, man is a reproducing organism. That
children should understand the basic principles of reproduction seems
critically important. Note that the writers are not confusing reproduction

with sex education. Sex education is a much broader amalgam of concepts than reproduction per se.

The examples stated above represent only a small number of those concepts which are often perceived as important from a literacy perspective. Others might include such things as evolution, work, the organism, population, community, ecosystem, pollution, time-space relationships, relativity, and theory.

(4) . . . understands and can use the science processes associated with basic inquiry or problem-solving strategies. When we speak of science processes we are dealing with those intellectual skills used by the scientist as he goes about the business of doing science. These processes are closely allied with what educators term "critical thinking". And, they probably have application (transfer potential) to all aspects of human activity which means that the processes of science can be used in problem solving activities beyond science. However, it may well be that science education can do a great deal to foster critical thinking in the human being and help students maximize their intellectual potential. This may well be the major contribution of science in the elementary school curriculum. Whether or not science contributes to critical thinking ability in students depends entirely on whether these thought processes are taught and, therefore, actualized. This is not an easy task but it is possible!

Because an entire chapter in this worktext deals with science process the writers will only provide a generalized description of these here. Science process includes such intellectual activities as observing, comparing, classifying, inferring, hypothesizing, designing and conducting experiments, predicting, and measuring. Those of you who learned in school that there was such a thing as a "scientific method" will be quick to note that many of these processes were referred to as part of that method. Today, however, most science educators take the position that there are many methods in science and that different scientific activities utilize different sets of processes.

(5) . . . appreciates and can apply the basic attitudes of the scientist. Certain values operate in science and these values are reflected in the more commonly held attitudes of scientists as they engage in research. Some of these values relate directly to the logic behind empiricism. Others are values held by the individual who is motivated to be involved in science itself. Basic curiosity is one of these and is closely allied to man's longing to know and understand. This attitude is often based on the premise that knowledge has value and that empirical inquiry should be undertaken to obtain that knowledge.

Another value is that associated with the demand for verification. A scientist often rejects knowledge that cannot be supported with hard data. At the very least, the scientist suspends judgment on a finding or theory until data are available which tend to reject said knowledge.

Most scientists have a sincere respect for empirical logic. Here the scientist insists that conclusions drawn from scientific work be based on a logical frame of reference with respect to available data. At the very simplest level, this characteristic is demonstrated by the insistence that an inference drawn from an observation be based on the logic of the situation rather than on intuition. In this way, scientific knowledge differs from dogmatic or intuitive knowledge. And, this is a difference that is critical to all of the activities of science. It is this, perhaps as much as any other single thing, that separates science from less empirical intellectual pursuits.

What is the Payoff for Literacy? Is There a Dividend for the Student?

Recently the writers of this worktext working with researcher H. G. Walding, asked over 200 professional scientists and science educators what they perceived the value of science education to be. Interestingly, their responses were not all alike. But, the majority of those who responded did so in one of two ways. Over 30% of all responding said that the value of science education lies in the critical thinking or reasoning dimensions of science. About 30% of those responding seemed to feel that the value of science education lay in man better understanding himself and/or the environment in which he lives. About 7% of those responding seemed to feel that science holds adjustment or survival potential for man and this is the major value. Other responses varied from gaining new knowledge, to enjoying a better and richer life, to the aesthetic or appreciation potential of science.

These responses would seem to indicate that the professionals who work in science feel strongly that both knowledge and process are big dividends for human beings in science education. The writers of your worktext would like to go one step further and state that knowledge and process without the application of these concepts and skills are probably of little value. The concepts, processes, and attitudes of science should serve as a firm foundation for attacking the many problems facing man today. Problem-solving is a very real need in today's society. The use of critical thinking skills, sound knowledge, and scientific attitudes can help every human being become more rational and, thereby, act as a force to liberate the human mind from the many debilitating constraints and liabilities imposed on it by cultural tradition and prejudice. Hopefully, to think and act rationally - without the blinders of sheer emotion operating to control behavior - will serve to emancipate the human spirit and, in the end, bring about behavior which results in increased human dignity.

Is there a Dividend for the Teacher?

In the opinion of the writers, there is about as much potential payoff for teachers in the teaching of science as there is for the students engaged in it. The unfortunate aspect of this opinion is that this payoff is often not identified by teachers and, therefore, remains unused in the classroom.

There is no question about the hard work involved for the teacher who teaches an experiential, hands-on science program for children. It is much,

much easier to ignore science or to relegate it to a "let's read about science" type program. For those teachers who are willing to expend the energy necessary to provide a hands-on program, there can be some ancillary payoffs that are extremely beneficial. A brief discussion of some of these follows. Several of these socalled payoffs will be dealt with in more detail later in the worktext.

An experiential science program is normally very <u>motivational</u> for students. This is understandable because in a hands-on situation students are "doing" instead of reading and/or writing about science. Since the modern science programs are highly inductive in nature, science is also a time of discovery or learning by doing. There is a definite motivational potential here for many students because they are actively involved in the learning process.

Teachers who have been teaching from the textbook and have, for one reason or another, switched to a hands-on approach, have found it difficult to return to the textbook as the principle focus for the science program. Once having experienced the doing of science, students are very reluctant to go back to a reading-oriented program.

Those teachers who make a practice of approaching the educational experience from an interdisciplinary perspective find that science content is an excellent vehicle for use in other content areas. Science as a <u>content vehicle</u> has potential for skill development in reading, language arts, and mathematics. Students are given an opportunity to draw upon their science knowledge for the development of experience charts in reading, various communication activities in the language arts, and in problem solving in mathematics. Because most children seem inherently interested in many science topics, they are prone to utilize these interests in the development of skills in other areas to a much greater extent than if the content used is of only a passing interest. Science subject matter is also generally free of age restrictions. Research tells us that young children are extremely interested in animals and that this interest tends to hold up well into the junior high school years. Other topics are also well suited for use as content vehicles, e.g., space exploration, fossils, prehistoric life, earthquakes and volcanoes, and reproduction in the later years. Teachers who supplement their regular textbook fare with reading, language, or math activities drawn from science are sometimes amazed to find that the children gain a vocabulary which would generally be thought to be much too advanced for students of their ages. Why would this be the case? Its probably a matter of the children understanding the concepts involved in the content being used. When this is the case, children are not normally too concerned about the difficulty level of the words involved. In other words, with respect to vocabulary, the children have intellectual "pegs to hang their memories on". In this situation, vocabulary development seems to become almost automatic instead of the typical drudgery so often associated with it.

We are reminded of the first grade teacher who was using fossils as a content vehicle in reading via the experience chart method. Her students had handled fossils and had seen a filmstrip on fossilization and how scientists went about the business of studying fossils. She reported that, during the writing of the experience chart, the students wanted to use the word "paleontologist" in their story. Further, she reported, "I would have used the word without hesitation except that I couldn't spell it."

The writers have already mentioned the transfer potential of those critical thinking skills that can be taught via science. For the teacher who is sincerely committed to teaching critical thinking, science may well be the one most important tool at her/his disposal. This is not because this is the only area in which critical thinking can be taught. It is simply because there are probably more programs available for doing this in science than in any other content area. Of major importance, however, is the very real potential for helping students learn how to transfer these skills to other content areas, e.g., social studies, language arts, math. The teacher who is teaching science process skills (critical thinking) in science and who helps students see how these same skills can apply to problem-solving situations in other content areas, is probably the teacher who is truly helping children become more proficient problem-solvers, i.e., critical thinkers. Therefore, the idea of teaching science process for the sake of science learning is only the beginning in the classroom where the teacher recognizes the need for critical thinking in other content areas as well.

In Summary Sound science instruction in the elementary school has pay-off value for both youngsters and the teacher. The major consideration for teaching science to children is something the writers term scientific literacy. In this context, however, literacy goes beyond the normal constraints placed on the term. Scientific literacy includes but is not restricted to elements like understanding science and the scientist, being able to differentiate between science and technology, understanding and being able to use the processes of science, and knowing and applying the basic attitudes of the scientist. Professional scientists and science educators believe that science education has value for training in critical thinking (reasoning), understanding self and the environment, and for helping man adjust to the universe in which he lives. With respect to pay-off for the teacher, science has potential for being very motivating, can be used as a content vehicle in other subject matter areas, and can serve as a model to be used to teach critical thinking which can be applied to all aspects of human endeavor.

The rapid progress true science now makes,
occasions my regretting sometimes that I
was born so soon. It is impossible to
imagine the height to which may be carried, in a thousand years, the power of
man over matter . . . O that men would
cease to be wolves to one another, and
that human beings would at length learn
what they now improperly call humanity.

        Benjamin Franklin - 1780

PART III

A Short History of Elementary Science Methods in the United States

Performance Objectives

Subsequent to your interactions with Part III, you will be expected to be able to . . .

1. . . . identify or define: (A) natural history, (B) anthropomorphism, and (C) teleology. Further, be able to explain the roles these have played (if any) with regards to religious education, object teaching, the Nature Study movement, and children's literature.

2. . . . compare and contrast (noting similarities and differences) the object teaching period in science education and the Nature Study movement.

3. . . . identify and/or describe those suggestions set forth in the early 1900's by Dewey and Craig which were aimed at improving elementary science education. Further, be able to explain the net effect these ideas had on actual in-class elementary science instruction.

4. . . . describe the impact of or identify the impact of the successful launching of Sputnik on science education in the United States.

5. . . . describe or identify the major goal(s) of the "big three" science programs funded by the National Science Foundation (N.S.F.). Further, be able to explain how these programs differ from traditional elementary science textbook programs.

6. . . . communicate the similarities and/or differences between the "big three" science programs and "second generation" elementary science textbooks.

7. . . . synthesize and communicate a succinct record of the major eras in science education along with the basic characteristics of each era.

---

* Part III was prepared by William J. Bluhm and constitutes a major revision of Part III of H. R. Hungerford and A. N. Tomera, Methods of Science Instruction for the Elementary School: A Worktext. Rantoul, Illinois: The Rantoul Press, 1974.

A Short History of Elementary Science Methods in the United States

In the Beginning –
The Didactic Era

The beginning of science education for children in the United States can be traced as far back as the late 1700's. Children's books, called the children's literature or the didactic literature, were the first method of elementary science education. These books were originally of British origin. Many of them were brought to the United States and were adapted to the new world and reprinted by American publishers.

The early American versions of the didactic literature had several purposes. One such purpose was to develop ethics, morals, and manners in youngsters. Within the stories children were shown the value of neatness, unselfishness, amiability, honesty, carefulness, etc. Another purpose of the children's literature was to stimulate the child to develop, on his own, some of the critical thinking skills such as observation, comparison, and experimentation. Transmitting scientific information, concepts, and principles from the written page to the child's head was yet another purpose of the didactic literature. Such topics as animals, plants, the solar system, seasons, and refraction of light were among those covered in the children's books.

Religious Influence on
Early Science Education

During the time that the didactic literature was being printed in the United States, religion was a dominating influence on people's lives. This domination was reflected in the children's literature. Children were taught a reverence for natural history, i.e., the objects and events of nature. Since God was the creator of the universe including all of the natural world, by developing a reverence for nature the youngsters would develop a reverence for God at the same time.

Additional religious influence of this era on the children's literature can be seen in terms of anthropomorphic and teleological references. The practice of tendering human characteristics to other life forms - anthropomorphism - was a common one. Thus references like the sly fox, the busy bee and the wise old owl crept into children's reading matter. Anthropomorphic references were to serve as models, after which children could pattern the building of their own characters. Another common practice of the era was to explain a phenomenon teleologically. That is, naturally occurring objects and events were explained in such a manner as to make the reader perceive that they were predestined to be that way. A tree, for example, grows where it does to provide shade for children. The cow is here to give milk for people to drink. The storm is God's will.

Even in present day literature, one can still find anthropomorphic and teleological references made to the objects and events of nature. However, the professional opinion today is to eliminate both from science literature because they tend to promote inaccurate and even debilitating conceptual perceptions of the universe.

The didactic literature, at its inception, was designed to be used by private tutors or parents who taught children at home. Financially, the children's literature was within the reach of only the upper classes. As time proceeded and the books were adapted for use in school classrooms, much of the scientific content was kept, but unfortunately development of the scientific skills such as observation and experimentation were emphasized less and less. The adapted books, as school materials, had become readers, the purpose of which was to transmit information, not critical thinking skills to the students.

Object Teaching   About the same time that the didactic literature was being adapted for classroom use (1860), the "object teaching" movement was beginning to sweep through Europe and the United States. This movement was started by Pestalozzi, a Swiss of Italian parents. A classic description of Pestalozzian object teaching is given by Krusi (7) when he states:

> To place objects before them (children) in which
> they are interested, and which tend to cultivate
> their perceptive faculties; and, at the same time,
> lead them to name the object, to describe its
> parts, and to state the relation of these parts.
> Thus language is also cultivated; and, from the
> observation of a single object, the pupil is lead
> to compare it with others, and the first steps in
> classification are taken.

In the United States the best known adaptation of Pestalozzian object teaching was developed at Oswego, New York. The newly formed National Education Association supported the Oswego object teaching and so it received nearly total acceptance across the country. Object teaching was based on a child's limitations rather than his capabilities. It was thought that elementary school children could think only in terms of the concrete, not the abstract. Further, it was believed that children could not interpret events or phenomena.

For its content, object teaching turned to the objects of natural history - rocks, minerals, plants, and animals. Objects, once placed before the children, were closely and continuously observed. Likenesses and differences were noted, described, and memorized. This was, therefore, an era in which description was the key element rather than interpretation or investigation into the cause and effect relationships of the universe.

Faculty Psychology -
The Basis of Object
Teaching   Object teaching was based on and supported by the principles of faculty psychology. "The emphasis on observation and memorization for very young children was based on the sequential development of capacities. It was falsely assumed that young children were able only to observe and identify objects but were unable to reason or to interpret phenomena". (10) Furthermore, faculty

psychology put forth the notion that the mind was a muscle that could be strengthened by exercise. Therefore, during the object teaching era, school children observed, compared, memorized, and described over and over again in an attempt to strengthen their brains.

As a method of teaching science, many contemporary writers come down hard on object teaching and its faculty psychology basis. Certainly, the psychological premise for object teaching was faulty. We know, for example, that children can intellectually manipulate basic principles of science and can interpret happenings and see relationships. Further, to focus solely on the strategies of object teaching is absurd from a general education point of view. Still, research indicates that the strategies of object teaching (critical observation, comparison, and communication) can help develop perceptual ability and, further, that these skills are retained over long periods of time and that these same skills can be transferred to new and unique situations. Thus the strategies of object teaching cannot be totally rejected for they may have some payoff value in terms of development and use of certain critical thinking skills.

Science Curriculum
Failures –

In the late 1800's, America was in the midst of industrial expansion. Citizens were viewing first-hand the practicability of new scientific information and its technological applications, e.g., railroads, agricultural machinery, telegraph, etc. As a result of science and technology's practical implications, citizens were demanding that the content of elementary school science be broadened and organized. The great interest that had been given to object teaching in the 1860's had begun to wane and with taxpayers calling for a new curriculum, object teaching began to fall by the wayside.

For about the next thirty years (1870-1900) prominent educators spent their time attempting to develop science programs. These programs tried to expand and organize science content. Further, these new science programs included the development of critical thinking and problem-solving skills. However, due primarily to the inability of teachers to handle these new science programs, they failed to become implemented.

The Nature-Study
Movement –

While the elementary science programs were failing, a new elementary science movement, the Nature-Study movement emerged in response to an industrial America. As large cities grew around booming industries, young rural adults were attracted by the employment, entertainment, and excitement the cities offered. A tremendous migration toward the cities took place with the attendant problems of city crowding and unemployment.

Nature-Study enthusiasts felt that if young children could be imbued with a deep appreciation of natural history they would not leave the farm for the city. Further, the Nature-Study movement was aimed at improving agricultural practices, thereby stimulating the rural economy. Centered at Cornell University and headed by Liberty Hyde Bailey, the Nature-Study

movement provided teachers with the materials they needed to successfully
teach about nature, i.e., Nature-Study manuals, supplementary readings,
and study guides.

The content of the Nature-Study science program was, like that of
object teaching, the things of nature. The material was, however, better
organized and more accurate. Although the Nature-Study's content was
sounder that that of the object teaching era, the method of instruction
was still that of object teaching based on faculty psychology. Observation,
comparison, memorization, and description were once again performed over and
over by students. Also, as before, the children were viewed in terms of
their limitations rather than in terms of their capabilities.

Nature-Study's aesthetic goal was to get children to love, respect,
and protect nature. To achieve this goal the Nature-Study movement
became interdisciplinary. Poetry, singing, painting, and writing were
incorporated into lessons. Whether the Nature-Study movement was successful
or not in saturating children with knowledge about and respect for nature,
the movement began to decline by the 1920's.

New Faces and
New Ideas –
During the second and third decades of
the 1900's, men of stature set forth
ideas that have affected elementary
science education to this very day. Dewey's ideas about elementary science
education were representative of his "learning by doing" philosophy. He
believed that scientific knowledge separated from the scientific processes
which generated that knowledge became, " . . . a body of inert information"
when presented to students. (4) Further, he pointed out that the method-
ology of science (science processes) was as of great, if not greater,
importance to the education of children than the knowledge of science.

In 1927 Gerald Craig (from Columbia University) published his dissertation Certain Techniques Used in Developing a Course of Study in Science for
the Horace Mann Elementary School. Craig's dissertation served as a focal
point for change in the American elementary school and many of these changes
can still be observed in curricula used by elementary school teachers. Craig
held that the elementary school science curriculum should deal with:

1. laws, principles, and concepts of science which
   are of immediate concern to the daily lives of
   people,
2. the health, safety, and economic aspects of
   science, and
3. the attitudinal dimensions of science.

Elements of Craig's philosophy continued to be expanded and developed by
science educators, including Craig himself, for many years. Over the years,
for example, the National Society for the Study of Education has published
several Yearbooks devoted to science education. The first was published in
1932 (the Thirty-first Yearbook) and others followed in 1947 and 1960.
Although science education was to become more sophisticated over the years,

Craig's initial thinking can be found reflected in each of these Yearbooks. Further, Craig served as senior author of one of America's foremost science textbook series until the beginning of the 1970's. Such was his impact and reputation.

The Shame of
It All -

Regardless of the impact made by Craig and others over the years, problems continued to plague science education. Although elementary school science should have been more attuned to the true cultural role of science, teachers walked into their classrooms across the nation, closed the classroom doors behind them, and proceeded to prostitute the very pedagogy which permitted their employment in the first place - a general education for all children. The science textbook became a reader and, where science activity existed, it existed largely for the sake of activity itself without any real concurrent inductive reasoning taking place. The entire premise for science in schools was somehow overlooked by poorly trained administrators, inept teachers, and economically oriented textbook publishers (most of which were completely unwilling to try and change the status quo). Science educators themselves failed to understand the realities of science and how children learn and, therefore, teacher training was only marginally effective as a stimulus for effective teaching.

Thus, for many years, elementary school children were short-changed and exposed only to a descriptive, deductive approach to science - and in some schools (and it continues even today) science was ignored completely. The very nature of science provides one of the most motivating of all tools available to the teacher and for decades educators were missing the opportunity to "turn kids on" to true intellectual development. We heard about the pedagogy of critical thinking and experiential learning but "fumbled the ball" at the classroom door.

The Spectre
of Sputnik -

On October 4, 1957 the Russian government pushed a satellite into orbit above the earth. The accomplishment of Sputnik instantaneously created chaos in political, scientific, and education circles. The prestige of the United States, at least in the minds of many leaders, was on the line. The accusation was made, immediately following Sputnik, that the schools in the United States were deficient in the teaching of science and mathematics (although, as J. Murray Lee (8) points out, when U.S. astronauts walked on the moon, no one rose up to give credit to the schools of the nation).

In any event, the Sputnik episode resulted in a deluge of strategies for improving science education - and other areas of the education system as well. The year following Sputnik saw the passage of the National Defense Education Act (NDEA). The NDEA was intended to help every American develop his skills and competencies to the fullest. The rationale for this strategy was to help the nation develop its manpower and insure the leadership essential for the preservation of demoncracy. (9) In accordance with these goals was the objective of improving instruction in such content areas as science, mathematics, geography, English, and reading. Monies were made available via the NDEA for the purchase of equipment, supplies, and instructional materials in these areas. Although many dollars did, in fact, serve to improve educational programs across the nation, much of the money was squandered with reckless abandon by school boards, administrators, and teachers who gave little thought to the educational needs of children and sound instructional programming.

Following NDEA, the Elementary and Secondary Education Act (ESEA) was passed in 1965. The ESEA covers a wide variety of education problems including the education of children from low-income families, improving school library facilities, the implementation of innovative curriculum programs, and supplementary strategies (e.g., instructional materials centers, educational T.V. programming, learning laboratories), educational research, and the operation of Research and Development Centers as well as Regional Educational Laboratories. In 1968, the Congressional budget for Title III of ESEA alone was $208,000,000. Such was the perceived need for the development and implementation of innovative educational projects.

In addition to NDEA and ESEA, both public and private agencies involved themselves in massive efforts to upgrade the teaching of science at both the elementary and secondary school levels. Of particular interest, are the contributions of the National Science Foundation (NSF). NSF has spent hundreds of millions of dollars subsidizing curriculum projects. The "Big Three" experiential elementary science programs developed with NSF funding were Science: A Process Approach (SAPA), Elementary Science Study (ESS), and Science Curriculum Improvement Study (SCIS). Although these programs differ in content, scope, and sequence, they are very similar in that each emphasizes the development of scientific processes or critical thinking skills in children. There are no textbooks to read; children engage in inductive activities in which thinking and doing give rise to intellectual skills and scientific information. In effect, children model the behavior of the scientist. That is, the children generate their own information by using the same intellectual skills that the scientist uses. However, the purpose of these programs is not to turn children into scientists, but to help children become critical thinkers and problem-solvers. In these experiential science programs the deductive, read-about-science method of textbook instruction gives way to the activity-oriented, inductive method of learning.

Second Generation
Elementary Science
Textbooks -
An outgrowth of the experiential elementary science programs of the 1960's are the "second generation elementary science textbooks" of the 70's. (5) A few of these new textbook series are the Ginn Science Program (GSP), Elementary Science Learning by Investigation (ESLI) and the Modular Activities Program in Science (MAPS). The thrust of these second generation texts is for the child to arrive at an understanding of scientific concepts by using the processes of science. The texts are designed to help the teacher engage the children in scientific investigations in which they develop and use their critical thinking skills to generate and understand

scientific information. Although they do contain a considerable amount of reading, these second generation textbooks are activity-oriented and inductive in nature. Taught properly, they are not a return to the read-about-science textbooks.

In Summary - Where Have We Been and Where Are We Going?

The present day experiential elementary science programs and second generation textbooks have come a long way from the didactic literature of the eighteenth and nineteenth centuries. Spanning the nearly two centuries since the didactic literature ushered elementary science into the United States, various movements and trends in science education have come and gone. The early trend toward classroom use of books which were adapted from the didactic literature was interrupted by the European-born object teaching movement. As object teaching faded and citizens demanded new science curricula, the first modern day thoughts were given to incorporating critical thinking and problem-solving skills into elementary science education. Unfortunately, teachers were unable to implement these new curricula and soon the Nature-Study movement, using object teaching and faculty psychology, was widely accepted. Following this movement, Dewey, Craig and others called for the incorporation of intellectual or critical thinking skills into elementary science education. Textbooks which emerged after Craig's dissertation, however, failed to become much more than science readers. Finally, the launching of Sputnik spurred the United States government to spend huge amounts of money on education. Some worthwhile experiential science programs were developed which were based to a large extent on helping children learn process or critical thinking skills. These experiential programs have been adapted and revised into the most current trend in the teaching of elementary science - that of the second generation elementary science textbook. The future trends in elementary science education will probably be, as past trends have been, reactions to historical events and movements or reactions to and outgrowths of preceding methods of elementary school science instruction.

References

1. Comstock, Anna D. Handbook of Nature-Study. Ithaca, New York: Comstock Publishing Company, Inc., 1947.

2. Craig, Gerald S. "Elementary School Science in the Past Century." The Science Teacher, Vol. 24, No. 1 (February 1957), 11-14.

3. Daniels, George H. Science in American Society. New York: Alfred A. Knopf, 1971.

4. Dewey, John. Democracy and Education. New York: The Macmillan Co., 1916.

5. Dyrli, Odvard E. "Is There Anything New About the New Science Textbooks?" Learning, Vol. 4, No. 5 (January 1976).

6. Hungerford, H. R. and Tomera, A. N. Methods of Science Instruction for the Elementary School. Rantoul, Ill.: The Rantoul Press, Inc., 1974.

7. Krusi, Hermann. Pestalozzi: His Life, Work, and Influences. New York: Wilson, Hinkle and Company, 1875.

8. Lee, J. Murray. Elementary Education Today and Tomorrow. Boston: Allyn and Bacon, Inc., 1972.

9. Piltz, Albert. "National Defense Education Act." Science and Children Vol. 2, No. 7 (April 1965).

10. Smith, Herbert A. "Historical Background of Elementary Science." Readings in Science Education for the Elementary School (Edited by Edward Victor and Marjorie S. Lerner, 1st Ed.). New York: The Macmillan Company, 1967.

11. Underhill, Orra E. The Origins and Development of Elementary School Science. New York: Scott Foresman and Company, 1941.

Food for Thought

Science teaches us that the universe is accessible to man's reason and that its functioning can be described by laws. This very knowledge is of immense value. For example: Fears, dread, and superstitions have been eliminated by just the knowledge that the heavenly bodies follow laws and that these bodies will repeat the past behavior invariably. Man is now the proud possessor of knowledge which enables him to view nature calmly and objectively. We breathe freely because we know that nature is not willful or capricious.

. . . An education in science prepares for citizenship in the very civilization which science has fashioned. . . . government is heavily involved with science in defense, communications, transportation, health and numerous other activities. The future citizen may be called upon even as a nonscientist to take a hand in these affairs. The citizen will have to vote on issues which involve science, and the citizen should know also what governments can do to support science. Many leaders are quite ignorant of what basic research is and how it leads to benefits for society. In particular they do not know the long road from pure science to technology.

Morris Kline - 1965

Science is the attempt to make the chaotic
diversity of our sense experience correspond
to a logically uniform system of thought.

Albert Einstein - 1940

PART IV

The Product Side of Science

Subsequent to your interactions with Part IV you will be expected to be able to . . .

1. . . . define scientific knowledge (product) as reflected in this section.

2. . . . define (or compare, noting important likenesses and differences) facts, laws, theories, and/or concepts in science.

3. . . . communicate the scientific value of theories and/or laws. Further, be able to communicate the educational implications of theories and/or laws.

4. . . . describe the utility (from an intellectual standpoint) of concepts in terms of their being:

       a.   a means of organizing information into mental categories or "packages of descriptions and relationships".

       b.   a way in which the human organism can analyze (mediate) new information in terms of what is already known about objects and events in the universe.

5. . . . describe how b. (above) is dependent on a. (above).

6. . . . explain why a broad range of accurate and fairly thorough concepts help a human being adjust to his environment.

7. . . . explain why a concept held by a human being can be accurate but incomplete.

8. . . . diagram and explain the inductive and deductive intellectual processes involved in concept formation and the use of concepts in mediating (processing) new information. You will be **expected** to use an example other than the ones used in this reading.

9. . . . define or describe both inductive and deductive intellectual reasoning and compare the two forms.

10. . . . explain why a science program totally devoted to the product side of science is an abdication of responsibility on the part of the elementary school teacher.

The Product Side of Science

Many of you who read this have experienced science in school from mostly a product standpoint. That is, in your science classes, the major component of science has been knowledge.

Today, of course, science educators feel that knowledge is not enough - that there is more to science and children should experience science in its full dimensions. Even so, knowledge in science is important even though teachers in classrooms should not rationalize a strategy for teaching only knowledge. It is unfortunate that, when product is emphasized, this dimension of science sometimes deteriorates into the learning of facts without any regard for concepts, attitudes, or intellectual processes.

What is knowledge? Knowledge in science includes all of those data that scientists agree to be true or that knowledge that scientists have generated which allows hypotheses to be formulated and tested. The important thing to consider is that knowledge (product) is produced in empirical ways which allow man to trust the products derived. Knowledge is, then, what man perceives as empirical truth - the stepping stones to a broader understanding of the universe - its objects and its events.

In general, knowledge in science might be described as a composite of facts, laws, theories, and concepts. The term data merely connotes those pieces or bits of information that are empirically derived and are the constituents of facts, laws, and theories. Concepts are a different matter - we would hope that they are supported by empirical data but, alas, often they are not and they become victims of ignorance and prejudice.

Fact In
Science

What is fact? A fact is merely something that is observable and/or measurable and which scientists agree is true. Facts are largely based on man's faith in empirical standards - the qualities of careful observation and standard measurement.

Nitrogen comprises 79% of the atmosphere. The density of gold in grams per cubic centimeter is 19.3. Ants have three distinct body parts. It is a fact that light travels at a speed of 186,000 miles per second. The speed of light has been measured. Scientists agree on the critical distance subsumed by a mile or a kilometer and they also agree on the interval of time known as a second. Once instruments are available for measuring how fast light travels it becomes a relatively simple matter to do so. Of paramount importance is for numerous scientists to be able to substantiate this finding. This is known as the scientific quality of replication. If an observation or a measurement cannot be replicated (repeated) it is mostly worthless. Of course, it might be worthy to the person who observed it but if it cannot be repeated publicly it is largely meaningless in science. To try to convince a scientist that a unique, private observation has scientific merit would be much like seeing a ghost and spending the rest of your life trying to convince your associates (or your psychiatrist) that you really did see this spectre and that it really exists.

Even though facts are important in science, they certainly are not ends in themselves. They play a much greater role in the formation of concepts or in serving as foundations for laws and theories in science. Unfortunately, in many classrooms, teachers act as though fact is a suitable end in itself. This is not a suitable approach to science with children. Facts tend to be forgotten quickly! Further, if facts cannot be related to a more important idea or used in a problem solving situation, they are of little value to the student.

What follows is a discussion of product components which have considerable implication for science education. The reader is asked to attempt to perceive the role fact plays in these products and to compare the intellectual value of these products to fact per se.

Laws   A law in science deals with a specific category of phenomena - it is a statement of a relationship between phenomena which appears to be invariable under the same conditions. Laws are the generalized statements of scientists which refer to particular records of scientific data which seem to indicate exact truths in science. One example would be the Law of Universal Gravitation.

Another example of a law is Gregor Mendel's Law of Segregation which refers to the sorting out and reappearing of seemingly lost recessive characters in the offspring of hybrids.

Mendel was a genius with plants and plant breeding. He noted, for example, that when he crossed short peas with tall peas that all of the offspring were tall. Thus, the short trait was apparently lost! However, when two hybrid offspring were crossed, the short (recessive) character reappeared in a ratio of 1 short to 3 tall. He found that one-fourth of the plants were pure tall, one-half were hybrid tall, and the remaining one-fourth pure short. Other traits in other hybrid crosses reacted in this same manner or ratio. This sorting out of genetic characters and their reappearance Mendel termed segregation; the principle involved became the Law of Segregation. Scientists have data from thousands of experiments that bear this out. Thus we have a law which states something about the happenings in nature. We put a high degree of trust in the law even though we cannot say that this will happen ever on end! The same holds true for the laws of physics or the other laws of biology. They fit the picture we have of the universe until something comes along to modify this picture.

There occasionally comes a time when something appears in science that causes a law to be changed. Such was the case with the Law of the Conservation of Matter. This law, simply stated, said that matter could neither be created nor destroyed. The writer memorized this law most carefully in high school and accepted its "truth" faithfully. Then came nuclear fission. We learned that matter can be transformed into immense amounts of energy, $E = MC^2$. We now, of course, do not accept the Law of the Conservation of Matter as stated above. Physicists do believe, however, that mass is universally conserved as a property of matter and energy combined.

We can see that <u>laws</u> are <u>principles</u> or <u>generalizations</u> <u>relating</u> <u>to</u> the <u>constants</u> or <u>regularities</u> <u>of</u> <u>happenings</u> <u>in</u> <u>the</u> <u>universe</u>. A law will allow us to predict what will happen under certain circumstances in the environ- ment. Laws are extremely valuable with the data that supports them. However, they are inductively derived and <u>no</u> inductive conclusion can have an absolute truth value because new data may eventually be found which will alter the conclusion and necessitate a new principle or generalization.

Theories   A <u>theory</u> <u>is</u> <u>a</u> <u>generalized</u> <u>statement</u> <u>which</u>
                                   <u>acts</u> <u>as</u> <u>an</u> <u>explanation</u> <u>for</u> <u>large</u> <u>numbers</u>
<u>of</u> <u>related</u> <u>facts</u>, <u>occurrences</u>, <u>or</u> <u>other</u> <u>phenomena</u> <u>in</u> <u>nature</u>. Loosely stated, a theory is a kind of hypothesis concerning observable and related phenomena. Theories result as an observer views the universe and perceives many different data that seem to have a relationship to each other. Theories are, of course, inductively derived.

Theories have come and gone in science down through the ages. Some have persisted and some have failed to meet the test of time as they were construc- ted on weak logic foundations. An excellent example of a poor theory was Lamarck's theory of evolution proposed in 1809. Lamarck attempted to explain evolution on the basis of the idea that changes in an individual could be brought about by influences in its environment and that these could be inherited.   This was saying, for example, that giraffes developed long necks by stretching them for food generation after generation. Today we know that this could not be the case. The facts of genetic evolution just do not fit the theory.

The Lamarckian theory of evolution changed many years ago due to the observations made by a gentleman by the name of Charles Darwin who took a world cruise on the H.M.S. Beagle. Darwin's observations on this voyage plus careful analysis of data afterwards resulted in a new theory of evolution, one which rocked the very foundations of the scientific community and one, by the way, which remains virtually unchallenged in the scientific community today. Simply, Darwin's theory was based on the idea of natural selection within breeding populations of organisms. The known facts of genetics, heredity, and adaptation bear out his thinking.

<u>Theories</u> <u>act</u> <u>as</u> <u>intellectual</u> <u>models</u> <u>for</u> <u>viewing</u> <u>the</u> <u>nature</u> <u>of</u> <u>the</u> <u>universe</u> (or a portion of the universe). These models provide a basis for scientific research. They pose a means of asking questions of the environment. Say, for example, that Lamarck's theory of evolution had received wide acceptance in the scientific community. Subsequent research into evolution would have been based on hypotheses related to that theory. Of course, eventually, scientists would have realized that Lamarck's theory (model) was unsound.

A good theory tends to be substantiated by research findings. And, this is the case with Darwinian evolution, an entirely different theoretical model.

Theories, like any other scientific model, do not have absolute truth value. We find certain exceptions to many theoretical models in science. Such is the case with the cell theory in biology and the theory of population dynamics in ecology. Even though these theories are not absolutes concerning the environment, they still serve as extremely valuable models for viewing the universe. We know, for example, that the germ theory of disease, developed by Pasteur in the 19th Century, is not 100% valid. Yet, it was a major scientific breakthrough at the time and, today, a century later, the germ theory of disease is an accepted model in research. Countless millions of human beings and domestic plants and animals owe their lives to a man who took time to view the universe with a different perspective.

Concepts   A very useful component of knowledge,
                                particularly in science education, is
the concept. Although many educational variations exist for definitions of concepts, an attempt will be made to keep the definition here as simple as possible. Let us refer to a concept as the mental image one has of an object or an event or the relationships that exist between objects and/or events.

Of prime importance is that a person's concept is his own - a private mental image generated from data fed into the intellect. This means that no one can speak or hear a concept! One can only communicate using language symbols to attempt to interpret a concept to another human being. Whether the human being subjected to the language input produces an appropriate concept is dependent on many factors.

One of these factors is the ability of the teacher and the learner to communicate effectively. Because concepts in science education are so terribly important, it becomes evident that the use of language in communicating concepts may be one of the poorest means of developing conceptual ideas in the minds of human beings. The potential for error is tremendous and this is one reason why we cannot refer to concepts as always being empirically derived. Indeed, they may be anything but empirical!

A person's concept of a portion of his environment is tempered by and a result of his experience background and the evidence at his disposal. A person with training in entomology certainly conceptualizes insects in a far different manner than a person with no training with respect to insects. The entomologist visualizes insects as a facet of the animal kingdom, classifiable, and of economic importance. The person with no training probably perceives many arthropods which are not insects as insects, sees no orderly manner in their classification, and relates them only to his own experiences, pleasant or otherwise.

It is obvious, then, that concepts can be erroneous - or correct but incomplete. The educational implications here are tremendous. An example of conceptual development might be beneficial and one can be found on the next page. Every intellectual discipline has a certain, organized structure

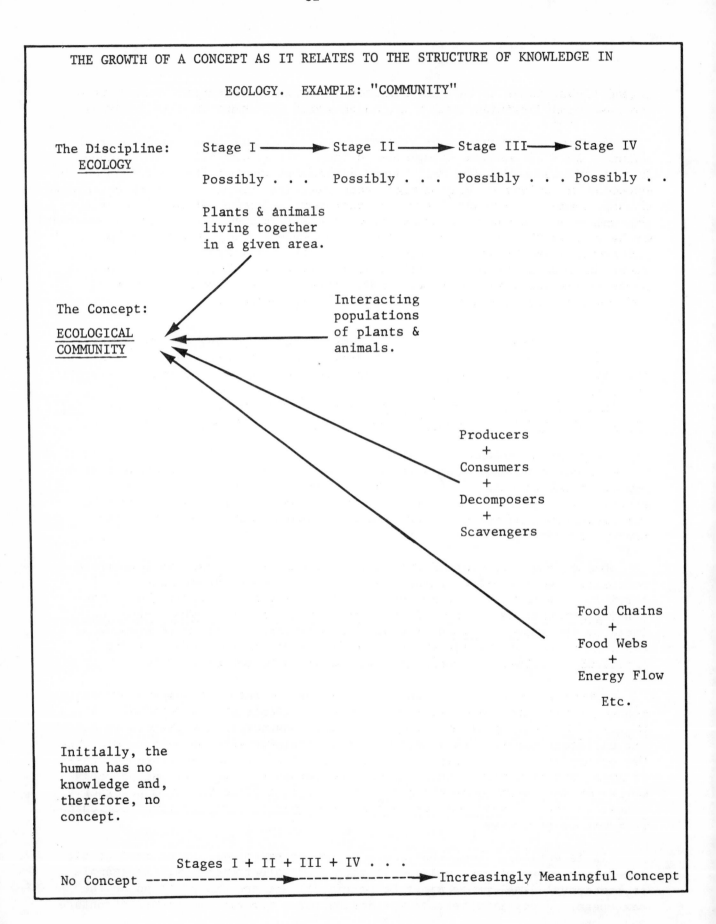

THE GROWTH OF A CONCEPT AS IT RELATES TO THE STRUCTURE OF KNOWLEDGE IN
ECOLOGY.   EXAMPLE: "COMMUNITY"

The Discipline:
ECOLOGY

Stage I ———▶ Stage II ———▶ Stage III ———▶ Stage IV

Possibly . . .   Possibly . . .   Possibly . . . Possibly . .

Plants & animals
living together
in a given area.

The Concept:

ECOLOGICAL
COMMUNITY

Interacting
populations
of plants &
animals.

Producers
+
Consumers
+
Decomposers
+
Scavengers

Food Chains
+
Food Webs
+
Energy Flow

Etc.

Initially, the
human has no
knowledge and,
therefore, no
concept.

Stages I + II + III + IV . . .

No Concept ----------------------▶---------------------▶ Increasingly Meaningful Concept

to its information. This structure facilitates the understanding of the
discipline and is often called the substantive structure of knowledge. In
the science of ecology, for example, the "community concept" has, for many
years, been a fundamental concept used in the interpretation of ecological
phenomena. In turn, the community concept itself is one with many bits and
pieces of information impinging on it. Needless to say, the more knowledge
a person has involved in his concept of "community", the more effective
or powerful the concept will be intellectually. In the presentation on the
prior page, we begin with a person who has no ecological community concept
(although he may have a well-organized cultural community concept). Over
time, this person's concept is broadened by the addition of new and unique
ideas concerning community structure and interaction. The presentation,
by no means, attempts to fully describe the variables operating in this
scientific concept but it does show how a concept can grow by the addition
of new information. It also helps one see how some of the inherent knowledge
in the concept might be organized.

Concepts are extremely useful in dealing with one's environment. They
help the individual cope with the universe in a logical and rational manner.
An example here might prove helpful. Let us reflect on the usefulness of a
correct and fairly thorough concept of "science" itself. The human being
with a faulty concept of science will often give to science almost omnipotent
powers - he will perceive science in an altruistic manner - he will
see science as being synonymous with technology - he will see the scientist
in a context which is almost totally foreign to the human one in which he
logically belongs. All of the above conceptual positions are faulty and could
prove ruinous to any large population of human beings holding tenaciously to
these ideas. The value of a correct concept concerning science and the
scientist is important to each human being. It permits the individual to
cope with science and society - as well as with his/her own social responsibilities - in a rational and productive manner rather than in a debilitating fashion.

Correct and usable concepts help a human being adjust to his environment.
Concepts are, in fact, means by which human beings organize knowledge into
useful mental categories or "packages of descriptions and relationships".
They also provide a basis for the logical mediation and interpretation of new
information as perceived by the individual.

As new data are brought into the mental patterns of the individual, they
are analyzed and interpreted in light of what is already known about the
objects and events of the universe. That is, available concepts are used to
determine if a reasonable interpretation can be made of the new information.
If the new data are seen as being related to the already held concept, the
data are integrated with the original concept and it is revised and/or
expanded to account for this new data. If a concept is not available which
allows for the interpretation of this data, a new concept must be generated
or the information remains uninterpreted. If data cannot be handled in some
logical manner, they remain as a discrepant event to the observer.

One can see that conceptual development is of critical importance to
the human organism if he is to be able to continually cope with all facets

CONCEPTUALIZATION - ROCKS

An Example of Inductive and Deductive Reasoning

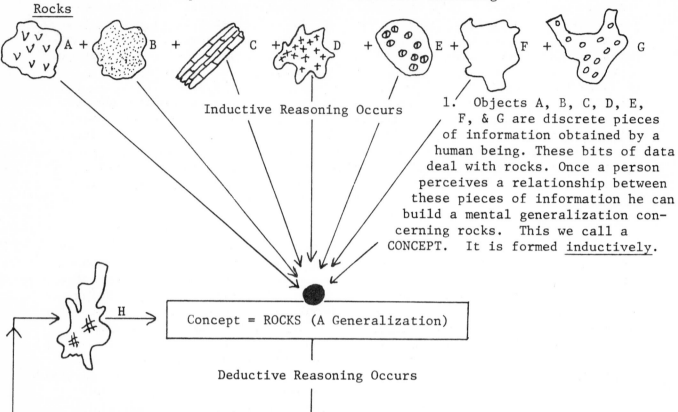

1. Objects A, B, C, D, E, F, & G are discrete pieces of information obtained by a human being. These bits of data deal with rocks. Once a person perceives a relationship between these pieces of information he can build a mental generalization concerning rocks. This we call a CONCEPT. It is formed inductively.

Concept = ROCKS (A Generalization)

Deductive Reasoning Occurs

3. Once the person has identified H as a rock (deductive reasoning), he can now use the new information obtained about H and revise his concept. Bringing H into the original concept is a matter of inductive reasoning and it produces a more complete concept concerning "rock".

Inductive Reasoning Occurs

2. Rock H is a new piece of information obtained by the human being after he has built his original concept. This rock has never been seen by the person before. However, due to the concept held, the observer identifies H as a rock. This is a mode of deductive reasoning.

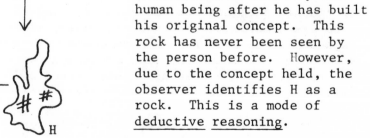

of his environment. And, the school is responsible for much of the conceptual growth of human beings.

One of the common complaints among teachers centers on the quality of concepts held by students in their charge. Students just do not understand this - or that - or the other thing! Of course its usually the former teacher's fault unless the child is a kindergartner and then the fault is the miserable experiential background provided by the parents! A rational look at these complaints points a finger of suspicion at the school itself and no teacher can avoid some responsibility for limited conceptual development in children. The school itself is organized in a manner which tends to force poor conceptual development in some areas. Teachers are likewise prone to use language symbols to the almost total exclusion of other methods in the development of conceptual ideas. This, of course, is a poor means of imparting accurate and thorough concepts.

Concepts are largely derived by the human intellect via inductive reasoning. Induction is a process whereby the person will pick up an assortment of separate pieces of information and put them together in some manner which makes them meaningful to the viewer. The individual generates a mental image which alludes to the relationships between these pieces of information. Of course, there has to be some connection between the bits of information - at least in the mind of the viewer. At any rate, this mental image is what we call the concept. Any new piece of pertinent information perceived by the person holding the concept can force a revision or expansion of the concept to make it even more meaningful.

Similarly, people use their concepts deductively. Deduction refers to the process whereby the intellect goes from the general (the concept) to the specific from a reasoning standpoint. A simple example would help here. All human beings have a concept of human being. All of us have been getting vast quantities of data concerning the human organism almost from birth. Therefore, the inductively derived concept of human being is fairly well established even in the minds of those unfortunate ones who come from poor gene pools. So what happens when you see a complete stranger on the street? You know almost instantly that this is another human being. You are, in fact, using your concept of a human being deductively here. Why don't you mistake this "animal" for a reptile, a bird, or an amphibian? It is simply because of your excellent concept of human being and your ability to identify even strangers as human beings. You do this deductively.

It may seem somewhat foolish to spend so much time here concerned with conceptual growth in a reading that is supposed to identify and discuss the product side of science. It is not foolish, however, because conceptual development is so tremendously important in science education and it behooves one to understand how it takes place. Also, the implications for science education (and other aspects of education as well) in terms of concept formation are apparent - students must be given as many opportunities as possible to deal with the objects and events of science on a first hand basis in order to develop truly meaningful and accurate concepts. It should be abundantly clear that personal experiences with objects and events are much more meaningful than surrogate experiences or language symbols. Similarly, the number and/or variety of experiences (as well as their accuracy) are important - one cannot form a good concept of insect, for example, by observing one insect. The same holds for any concept that is important to human beings.

In Closing . . .   This, then, is the product side of
                        science. We have briefly explored the
characteristics of the facts, laws, theories, and concepts in science. Their importance cannot be underestimated. Even so, to approach science education from totally a product standpoint is to abuse and misinterpret the discipline and withhold from children one of the most important things that science has to offer - the development of critical thinking and the human intellect!

The fundamental characteristic
that is common to both children
and science is that both are
actively involved in interpreting the objects and events
of the environment.

Gerald S. Craig

PART V

The Process Side of Science

Performance Objectives

Subsequent to your interaction with Part V you will be expected to be able to . . .

1. . . . logically defend the following statement: In order to maximize a human being's ability to think critically, education must provide him with operational models of specific intellectual skills and offer him opportunity to use these in as many different situations as possible.

2. . . . explain how science education offers a powerful educational vehicle for teaching critical thinking skills.

3.(*) . . . demonstrate your ability to make scientific observations. Further, you will be expected to be able to identify which senses you used in making discrete observations . . . and, to classify observations as qualitative or quantitative.

4. . . . operationally define the science process of classification.

5. . . . cite at least two functional, cultural uses of classification other than formal scientific taxonomy.

6. . . . defend the basic assumption that classification schemes depend largely on a person's perspective of his universe (or immediate needs).

7.(*) . . . formulate and defend an alternate and logical classification scheme for a set of previously classified objects.

8. . . . operationally define and distinguish between the following five terms: (1) observation, (2) conclusion, (3) inference, (4) hypothesis, and (5) experiment.

9. (*) . . . demonstrate the ability to transfer the ability to use a science process to a new and unique situation.

10. . . . explain how the inferring process is related to a person's personal perceptions of the environment as well as knowledge held concerning the environment.

11. (*) . . . prepare logical inferences based on observations of physical phenomena.

12. (*) . . . write increasingly accurate inferences based on the acquisition of new information.

13. (*) . . . write logical hypotheses which are consistent with the scientific parameters of the hypothesis.

14. (*) . . . produce testable, written hypotheses based on observations of physical phenomena.

15. . . . explain why the hypothesis serves as the focal point of scientific research.

16. (*) . . . prepare a generalization concerning physical phenomena based on the interpretation of recorded data.

17. (*) . . . successfully transfer descriptive and tabular data to a graph.

18. (*) . . . produce a logical, written conclusion based on ecological data.

19. (*) . . . prepare logical, written inferences based on ecological data.

20. . . . describe or identify the difference between dependent and independent variables.

21. (*). . . demonstrate the ability to control and manipulate variables in an experimental setting so that a hypothesis can be tested.

22. . . . analyze the pendulum process activity and identify those discrete science processes used in that activity.

23. . . . analyze any of the process models used in this chapter and describe how that activity supports the concept that science is a combination of process and product.

   (*) - Objectives which will be demonstrated specifically as a part of laboratory or interpretive work done in class. The student should also be able to use these same processes on a quiz in a transfer situation.

An hypothesis is, strictly speaking, a proposition which is put forward for consideration, and concerning the truth or falsity of which nothing is attested until the consideration is completed. It is thus necessarily associated with doubt, but with doubt of a negative rather than a positive kind. With the doubt which consists of a suspense of judgment rather than with the doubt which consists of an inclination to disbelieve.

Norman R. Campbell - 1922

The Process Side of Science

The process side of science deals specifically with the doing aspect of science - the use of intellectual skills to obtain answers sought from the universe. Whether the process is used by a child making a simple observation of a part of his environment or an astronomer searching for evidence of celestial bodies not revealed by photographs, it makes no difference as long as the investigation is empirical. The simplest critical observation may yield data just as the most complex experiment. Knowledge of hypothesizing and inferring may well help a student to cope more successfully with many situations that seem to demand problem solving skills. Knowledge of what constitutes a rational conclusion or a logical recommendation may influence a person's decision-making in a fruitful direction rather than a debilitating one. Herein lies one of the prime reasons for helping children achieve the skills of scientific inquiry - an ability to think critically may be the most liberating phenomenon of man's culture.

Should the reader find this defense for teaching science process unacceptable, perhaps a brief commentary in terms of an anecdotal defense for process education would be appropriate. Earlier we discussed the business of inductive and deductive reasoning, themselves examples of thinking processes. In the same context, emphasis was placed on concepts and conceptualization and the argument established that legitimate concept development served the individual in enabling him to mediate stimuli impinging on his senses from the universe around him. The entire business of inductive conceptualization is, itself, a highly functional form of classification. Classification is, further, one of the basic process components of science. Man uses certain kinds of classification skills each and every day of his life.

If man is so proficient in the use of classification in concept formation, why should we bother to promote its inclusion in science education? But, wait, who said that man was able to maximize his classification ability automatically? Indeed, we have evidence to support the notion that he cannot! Further, we have considerable evidence to support the idea that man increases in his ability to classify when he better understands the constructs of classification itself. Education can help him do this - and quickly and efficiently as well! If that isn't enough, we also have evidence to support the contention that man's ability to classify is increased when we specifically train him to sharpen his cognitive powers of observation and comparison. Why? Because these are basic and simple prerequisites for effective and empirically defensible classification behavior.

Similarly, there is considerable evidence to support the assumption that, once a person has had training in a specific aspect of problem solving, he can transfer this cognitive ability to a new dimension, particularly if the new situation appears to necessitate the same kind of thinking as that on which training was conducted. Further, modern educators of repute believe firmly that the student can be specifically taught mechanisms for transferring critical thinking that permit him to apply his ability to a wide range of new and unique situations.

If we were to generalize a statement of paramount importance concerning the development of critical thinking skills it would be as follows: In order to maximize a human being's ability to think critically, education must provide him with operational models of specific intellectual skills and offer him opportunity to use these in as many different situations as possible.

Modern science education offers one of the most powerful vehicles available for teaching critical thinking skills. This does not mean that other disciplines lack this opportunity. Science education, however, has brought process to the forefront and has designed both simple and complex vehicles for teaching cognitive skills. Hopefully, all other disciplines will eventually provide an equally significant emphasis.

In this chapter you will be introduced to a variety of specific science processes. In addition, you will have an opportunity to apply these skills in science situations. These, plus other activities later in this worktext, should provide you with a foundation for helping children in classrooms across the nation become better critical thinkers. Hopefully, you will approach these exercises with that idea in the forefront of your mind.

At the earliest level of instruction, the individual needs to learn how to observe, how to figure, how to measure, how to orient things in space, how to describe, how to classify objects and events, how to infer, and how to make conceptual models. These capabilities he will use all of his life.

Robert M. Gagne

An Observation Process Model

Critical observation and the subsequent correct and careful communication of observations made are the most powerful tools of the scientist.
Observation and communication skills are used in a wide variety of ways in
science. Further, they are integral parts of other processes as well, e.g.,
both play important roles in experimentation.

This activity is designed to introduce you to the skills of observation
and accurate communication as well as give you some practice in making
critical observations.

You will be given a candle and matches. Please place a drop of wax
on the surface in front of you and affix the bottom of the candle to it.
Next, light the candle. If you have long hair, be very careful to keep
it away from the flame.

In the space below, please record all of the discrete critical
observations you can make relative to the burning candle.

My List of Critical Observations

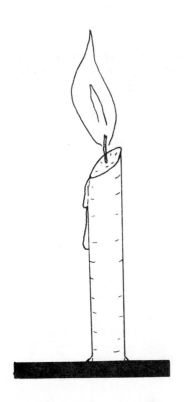

Analyzing Your Observations

One of the most common errors associated with students who are making scientific observations is that of slipping in a few "observations" which are really inferences. An observation in science can only be that which is <u>directly available</u> to the observer through one of his senses. Any interpretation of an observation goes beyond this and must be called an <u>inference</u>.

Please go back to your original list and cross out any "observations" which are, in reality, inferences.

Now that you have a final list of sorts, you might find it interesting to inspect your list to determine which senses were used in making your observations. As you know, the senses are sight (S), touch (T), hearing (H), smell (Sm), and taste (Ta). Why don't you <u>code each observation</u> on your list according to the sense used in making each observation?

Do you observe that you used one sense more than any other? Which one?

Sense used most: _____ Why?

Explanation:

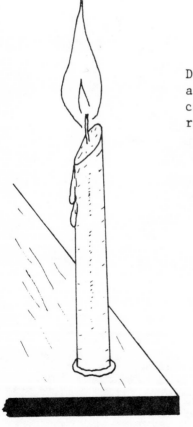

Do you think that you could now go back and produce a more thorough list of observations on the burning candle? Want to try again? Why not! Prepare a revised listing below:

List, Continued:

Now that you have a revised list of observations, there is one more analysis task for you. Observations can be either qualitative or quantitative. A qualitative observation is one which is descriptive in nature; it involves quality rather than quantity. A quantitative observation, on the other hand, involves some measurement of quantity or amount.

Return to your revised list and code your observations as to whether they were qualitative (Ql) or quantitative (Qt). What does this analysis show? Why do you suppose this is the case?

44

A Classification Process Model

The world in which we live contains quite a variety and number of living and non-living things as well as events. As man observes these things, he notices that many of them are alike while others are very different. In other words, man <u>compares</u> the things which he observes. A step subsequent to this observation and comparison is the separation of these objects or events into groups that contain closely related items (sharing of a large number of similarities). His purpose in classifying is probably twofold: (1) to impose an order on the objects and events of which he is aware, and (2) to allow him to use his knowledge of the universe more easily.

Since the methods of classification are man-made, one must realize that any such system is arbitrary in nature. Its validity rests on its acceptance by the rest of society and in classification in science, with agreement of the scientific community. Classification takes place in other facets of life besides science. Grocery and department stores are examples of man's classification ability. So are newspaper want ads and the yellow pages. Each is useful yet arbitrary. Each classification system which man creates is based on a logic pattern with which man's mind can cope. These systems are arbitrary yet they are accepted because they are based on an orderly thinking pattern which is supported by the observations and comparisons man makes on any set of objects and/or events.

Most objects and/or events can be classified in more than one way as long as the classification construct fits the data. For example, an entomologist might classify insects on the basis of their body structure (anatomy) whereas an agriculture expert would classify them as being beneficial, harmful, or neutral in regards to man and man's domestic plants and animals. A member of some anti-defamation league might classify movies in terms of their redeeming social value whereas someone else might classify them in terms of their subject matter, e.g., western, science fiction, musical.

In summary, classification systems are created by man to help him intellectually organize his knowledge. Classification systems are arbitrary and are acceptable only if they are logical and fit the data available to the classifier. Classification systems for the same objects and/or events may vary, usually in terms of the needs of the individual.

Classifying Cheerleaders!   Few people would take the time or energy to classify objects like cheerleaders.   But, for our purposes here they seem like a good and fun way to begin classifying. On the next page you will find eight (8) good-looking college cheerleaders. You will also find that they have been classified (categorized) three separate times. Each time they were classified, the classification system becomes more refined. This particular system is referred to as a three-stage classification scheme. There could have been fewer or more stages. Please observe and compare these cheerleaders and then study how they have been classified. Then, reclassify the third stage of cheerleaders into another third stage - a new one. Remember that your new third stage must be logical and defensible on the basis of available data!

CLASSIFYING CHEERLEADERS

First Stage Classification

| 1, 2, 3, 4, 5, 6, 7, 8 |

All Cheerleaders

Second Stage Classification

| 1, 2, 3, 4 | | 5, 6, 7, 8 |

Males   Females

Third Stage Classification

| 1, 4 | 2, 3 | 5, 7 | 6, 8 |

Right Hand Up   Left Hand Up   Right Hand Up   Left Hand Up

How else might the third stage be classified?

DO IT! What observable evidence do you have that will defend this new third stage?

More Information
About Classification!

Far too many people, when they are beginning to learn the basis of classification, think that the second and third stages must be divided into groups that contain **equal** numbers of items. This was exactly the case with cheerleaders. This idea about classification is not correct, however. There are many times when the classification scheme looks quite a bit different than it did for the cheerleaders.

Let's take a look at one example of a classification scheme in which the second and third stages don't look as they did with the cheerleaders. In this particular situation we are grouping geometric shapes into a logical but arbitrary system. What are the characteristics of the second and third stages?

Classifying Geometric Shapes

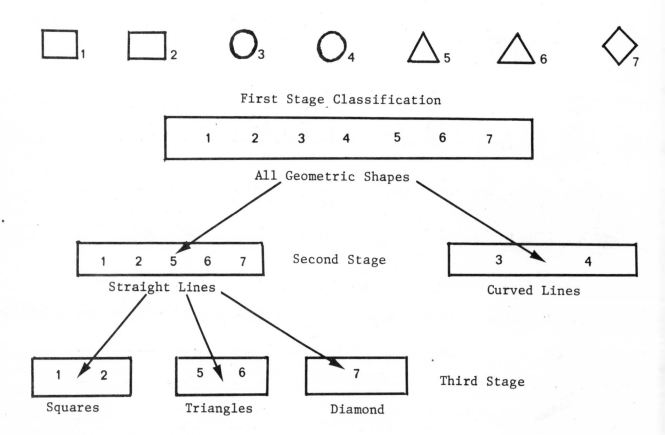

First Stage Classification

All Geometric Shapes

Second Stage

Straight Lines

Curved Lines

Third Stage

Squares   Triangles   Diamond

Twig
Classification
Task

In Appendix A can be found twelve (12) line drawings of twigs from trees in winter condition. Trees are much more commonly classified than cheerleaders. Your task will be to construct a three stage classification scheme for these winter twigs.

Although classifications are but arbitrary schemes through which man organizes knowledge they must also be logical and useful. Therefore, the degree to which your scheme is correct reflects the extent to which it is logically and accurately based. Similarly, this logic must be communicable and acceptable to others.

Please classify the winter twig drawings below. Use only the physical characteristics observable in the drawings. Fig. 1 in Appendix A may help you in identifying the names of some of the structures you observe on the twig drawings. Disregard the length of the twigs. Be careful to list the characteristics you used for each stage in order to defend your classification scheme. When you are finished, please to to the next page.

Twig Classification System

Defend your classification scheme here:

A Possible
Answer!

Twigs

First Stage: 1,2,3,4,5,6,7,8,9,10,11,12

Second Stage: 3,6,9,10,12   1,2,4,5,7,8,11

Third Stage: 3,6,9   10,12   1,7,11   2,4,5,8

Fourth Stage: 1   7   11   5,8   2,4

Rationale:

First Stage: All Twigs!

Second Stage: 3,6,9,10,12 -------- Opposite leaf scars!
                  1,2,4,5,7,8,11 ----- Alternate leaf scars!

Third Stage: 3,6,9 --------------- Small leaf scars, few bundle scars!
                  10,12 -------------- Large, U-shaped leaf scars, many
                                       bundle scars in a pattern!
                  1,7,11 ------------- Self-pruned (no terminal bud)!
                  2,4,5,8 ------------ Terminal bud present!

Fourth Stage: 1 ----------------- Rounded leaf scar and circular,
                                       light-colored pith!
                  7 ----------------- Leaf scars surrounding the buds;
                                       angular pith!
                  11 ---------------- Heart-shaped leaf scars; round,
                                       dark-colored pith!
                  5,8 -------------- Single terminal bud at tip of twig!
                  2,4 -------------- Cluster of buds at tip of twig!

Inferring Process Model

A few years ago, a fireworks manufacturing plant blew up and burned in northeastern Illinois. This phenomenon produced some interesting inferences. One woman who lived near Chicago and heard the explosion later told newsmen that she thought (inferred) that she was hearing a sonic boom at the time of the explosion. A well known Chicago T.V. weatherman observed, from a distance, the huge cloud that formed above the factory. He admitted on T.V. that he had inferred that the cloud was of meteorological origin and had failed to figure out how this one cloud had developed on such a clear day.

Such is the state of affairs with inferences. An inference is an explanation of an observation. How an observation will be interpreted (or explained) is based largely upon a person's background of experiences and the logic used in the interpretation. Both the housewife and the weather man made inferences about the fireworks factory explosion based on their own background of experiences - their individual frames of reference.

The weatherman was all too "human" in that he avoided a basic principle of inferring in science. He should have drawn as many logical inferences as possible. If he had done this, he might have had two or more inferences from which to choose. He might have concluded, after all, that the "cloud" might be more logically explained on the basis of fire/explosion than on meteorology (particularly on a day when there wasn't a cloud in the sky).

In science, inferring can be a fundamental tool of the scientist. It is used - and has been used historically - to direct the observer in producing new information. There are some classic cases where inferring has had great pay-off value. Think for a moment where we might be today medically if A. Fleming had not inferred that the Penicillium mold, growing in his bacteriological plates, was inhibiting the growth of bacteria. It is more than interesting to note that this same observation had been made before by others but that it was largely ignored. Fleming's inference led to a testable hypothesis which led to the isolation of penicillin in the 1930's.

It is critically important to differentiate between an observation and an inference. A scientific observation is empirical data brought into the mind through one of the senses. The observation is available to anyone in the right place at the right time with his/her perceptive faculties turned on. The inference, however, is much more private - it is an intellectual explanation of the observation.

You walk out of the theatre one summer night and the streets are wet. This you observe. Your inference? Of course, it rained! Which is hard data? Which is intellectual speculation? Enough said!

Inferring Exercise 1.   On the next page you will find two line drawings. Part A represents a demonstration in progress. A glass bowl has a burning candle attached to its center. About

75% of the bowl is filled with water. A glass (or plastic) cylinder is about to be inverted over the candle into the water. The cylinder is closed at one end.

Part B represents the completed demonstration. The candle is no longer burning. The cylinder is about 20% filled with water. The water level has also gone down in the bowl.

The line drawing represents recorded data (observation). And the inference? Just what could one infer from the observed phenomena? It might be logical to infer that the water level has risen inside the cylinder because the oxygen (O_2) was used up during combustion. This is not entirely illogical because we know that the atmosphere is nearly 20% oxygen. How good an inference is this? Are there others? We think it only fair to permit you to replicate (repeat) this demonstration, make critical observations, and then judge the value of the above inference.

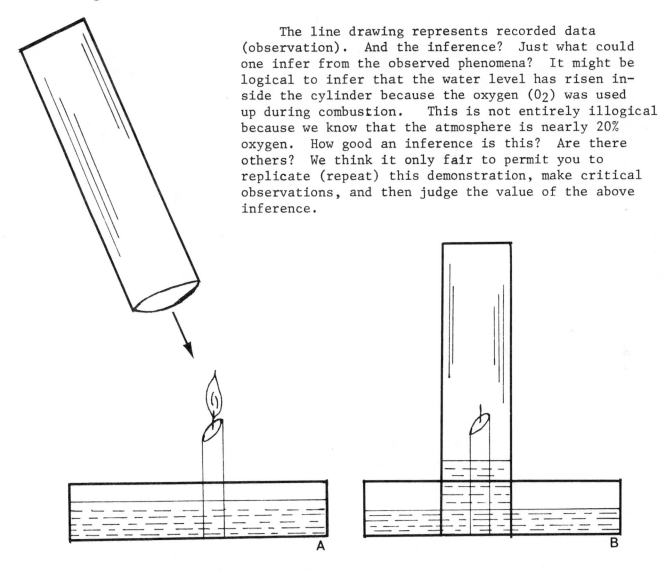

Necessary materials will be provided so that you can replicate this demonstration. Please make <u>careful</u> <u>observations</u> throughout the <u>entire</u> process. List all discrete observations below:

Observations, continued:

From the observations made, what inference seems most logical? Are there two? Or more? Space has been provided below for your statement of the inference(s). If there is more than one, asterisk (*) the one that seems best.

Can you think of any way to test your preferred inference? How would you go about it? We are not going to ask you to test your inference but, if you did choose to test the inference, it would become a hypothesis. Why? Because a hypothesis is a testable generalization based on observations and/or inferences about observations. More on this later!

53

Inferring   This exercise will not only help demonstrate the
Exercise 2.   process dimension of inferring, it will show the
                        value of data available to the observer, i.e.,
knowledge held by the observer influences the quality of inferring. We
ask that you give this activity your "intellectual all".

On the following page you will find a photo. Here is some information
concerning the scene at which you are looking:

     This photograph was taken in August, high in the San Juan
     Mountains of southern Colorado. The observer is looking into a
     huge rock-lined amphitheater. Snow still remains on the slopes
     of the mountain. Huge deposits of soil and rock lie piled up at
     the foot of the rock walls which form the amphitheater. Immense,
     angular rocks lie scattered around within the amphitheater. Grass
     and alpine wild flowers cover the ground. If you look closely
     near the center of the photograph you can see a man sitting with
     his back to the photographer. He is seated on one of the smaller
     rocks found here.

Your task? Prepare an inference to account for the presence of the
huge, angular rocks seen scattered about within the amphitheater. Write
your inference below:

55

Don't be too frustrated if you feel you didn't do too well coming up
with a reliable inference. We wonder how well you could do with some additional information. Here is that information:

   The San Juan Mountains have experienced long periods of
   glaciation. About 100,000 years ago, the North American climate
   was much colder than today. Snow piled up in the mountains each
   year and large amounts did not melt. The unmelted snow turned to
   ice as more snow accumulated on top of it. Over the years, thick
   glaciers formed and these moved down the mountains to resculpture
   the landscape.

   High on mountain tops the glacier carved huge amphitheaters
   out of solid rock. These amphitheaters are called cirques and
   are known as the birthplace of valley glaciers. Cirques are
   visible over much of mountainous North America and Europe.

   Glacial ice will accumulate to depths of hundreds of feet
   inside a cirque. As it grows in depth it also moves slowly out
   of the cirque and down the mountain slopes. Valley glaciers are
   thus formed.

Your task? Prepare a new and better inference using the new knowledge
now at your disposal. Write this inference below:

Could you use still more information in accounting for the huge, angular rocks seen scattered about within the cirque? Maybe your inference would be even better given additional information. Here it is:

> As ice forms at the rear of a cirque, some of it becomes frozen to rock fragments on the wall of the cirque. As the glacier moves slowly out of the cirque, the ice may actually "pluck" these rock fragments out of the side of the mountain and carry them along.

> Rock fragments that have been moved long distances usually have a rounded appearance. Those that have traveled short distances usually have an angular appearance. As the years passed in the San Juan Mountains, the climate warmed. Eventually, the glaciers melted and disappeared from this mountain range.

Your task? Prepare your final inference using your observations of the photo and all accumulated knowledge. You should find this stage of inferring to be fairly easy. Further, you should have a high level of confidence in this, your last inference. Why?

Write this last inference below:

Do you feel more comfortable with your last inference than you did with either the first or the second? If so, why? Would it appear that a person's knowledge or concepts affect his ability to successfully infer?

In the specific problem revolving around glaciers, cirques, and angular rocks you may wonder whether it would ever be possible to test such an inference. In fact, it is very possible! How? Earth scientists attempt to interpret the past by observing present events. They travel to a point on the earth's surface where glaciation is active today and carefully observe the associated phenomena. It is a fairly simple matter to find analogies between present observations and evidence remaining from the past. Such is the case here. The earth scientist will readily tell you that understanding the present is the key to interpreting the past! This is an accepted assumption in the field of earth science.

Hypothesizing Process Model

A hypothesis is sometimes defined as a testable generalization based on observations and/or inferences about observations. Hypotheses are widely used in all facets of science, i.e., physical science, behavioral science, etc.

Assume that you are a sixth grade teacher who is also interested in doing educational research. Your observations of sixth grade students seem to infer that they are, many times, motivated to learn for the sake of grades. You ponder this and decide to enlist the help of a number of fifth, sixth, and seventh grade teachers in conducting an experiment to test your inference. Your research hypothesis might read as follows:

> Research Hypothesis: Middle school students will perform significantly better when extrinsically motivated by grades than students who have no such external motivation for learning.

The above hypothesis generalizes to middle school students and is designed to test an inference. Further, it is testable in a number of different ways. Thus, it fits the definition for a statement of a hypothesis.

Let's assume also that you are a physical science student. Your investigations into solar radiation seem to indicate that dark soils reach a higher temperature during daylight hours than lighter colored soils. It would appear that this could lead to a worthwhile generalization (concept) in science. Try your hand at writing a hypothesis for this situation that follows the rules for hypothesizing.

Proposed Hypothesis:

Please check your hypothesis against the definition read earlier and also with your instructor. If it needs revision, prepare a new hypothesis below:

Now, we are going to put you into the real, three-dimensional world of hypothesizing. Follow instructions carefully!

Hypothesizing   For this activity you will need one
In Earnest!   30.5 cm ruler (centerpunched), two
                       coins of equal denomination, an
assortment of other coins, paper or cardboard, and a pencil. In this
activity you are going to observe the effect of gravity on falling bodies,
e.g., coins. Before you can do this effectively, however, you must develop
some psychomotor skills.

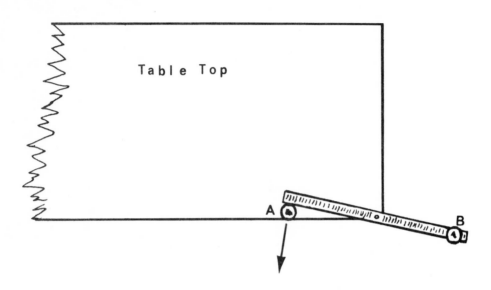

        Using a table top, ruler, and two coins of equal denomination, set
up the demonstration as you see it in the drawing above.

        Using your middle finger, flick the ruler in such a way as to force
coin A off the table and coin B off its station on the ruler. This can be
difficult to accomplish at first so practice until you have the technique
down pat. When you have polished your technique, the results you obtain
will appear to be something like the following:

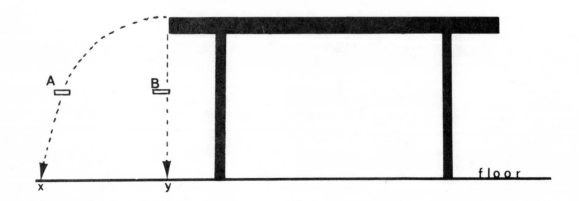

When you have the procedure down pat, record your observations of the phenomenon as it relates to the "behavior" of the two coins.

Observations:

Now, try the same procedure with two identical coins of a different denomination. For example, you might use two half dollars. Observe carefully what happens.

Does a hypothesis come to mind? One should! It should relate to a generalization concerning the phenomena you have observed. Write this hypothesis below:

Hypothesis 1:

The following represents one possible hypothesis for the above events: Objects of equal mass, whether dropped or pushed from equal heights, will hit the floor at the same time.

Is the hypothesis testable? How would you go about testing it? Think of specific ways of testing your hypothesis.

Now, let's modify the situation slightly. Repeat the demonstration using coins of two very different masses, e.g., a quarter and a dime. What do you observe the results to be? Repeat the procedure a second - even a third or fourth time. Was the original hypothesis a good one? Did it account for enough variables? If not, revise the original hypothesis below:

Hypothesis 2:

Is Hypothesis 2 testable? Does it follow the rules for hypothesizing? Think of specific ways of testing this hypothesis. You might, for example, want to use entirely different objects this time. Think of some possibilities. Test Hypothesis 2.

The variables tested for Hypothesis 2 should eventually lead you to another revision of the hypothesis. If your inferences are based on all possible data and if you have used good logic in forming your inference(s), you will be forced to write a hypothesis that could be tested but only in a more sophisticated laboratory than the one in which you are working. How would that hypothesis read?

Hypothesis 3:

It should be obvious, at this point, that hypotheses are somewhat similar to inferences. They are, in fact, very special kinds of inferences about the universe. Further, they must be testable and they should relate to some generalizable principle or concept. Even though a research hypothesis may not prove itself to be correct, it still functions as a focal point of research. In the end, the hypothesis is accepted, rejected, or revised.

A Hypothesizing Problem Involving Transfer –

Hypothesizing is a science process and definitely a component of critical thinking. As such, the skill itself should be generalizable to new and unique situations. As an elementary teacher, you will be expected to successfully teach several content areas besides science, e.g., language arts, math, and social studies. Should critical thinking apply to these areas as well? Indeed, it should!

Your task here is to describe a real or hypothetical classroom situation where hypothesizing could be a valuable educational tool in a content area other than science. The situation should probably be a problem setting in a particular content area. For example, it might deal with the relationship that seems to exist between human values and vandalism or littering in the community. The children may not be able to test the hypothesis directly but it should be one that can be tested somewhere in the culture and one that the students can discuss. Give this task a try below:

Hypothesis:

Interpreting Data

Interpreting   On the next page you will find a graph
Sunspot Data.   which portrays the annual sunspot numbers
                                between 1935 and 1966. Sunspot data, like
so many other data, help generate the scientific assumption that happenings
in the universe are mostly goverened by laws and that events are not capricious
and unpredictable, i.e., scientists believe that there is order in the universe.

What kinds of information can be generated by a careful interpretation
of data such as that found on the graph? First, what do the data between
1935 and 1966 suggest? Record your interpretation below:

Interpretation of sunspot data:

Second, is it possible to predict sunspot activity beyond 1965 as a
consequence of looking at available data? We know, for example, that when
sunspot activity is high, certain kinds of communication devices do not work
well. At the time of this writing (November of 1976), scientists are predicting
that by 1978 C.B. radios will be increasingly difficult to operate with confidence due to increasing sunspot activity. It is a well-known fact that C.B.
radios don't work well at all during times of intense sunspot activity. From,
the data you have available, is the 1978 prediction a reasonable one? Why?

Answer:

65

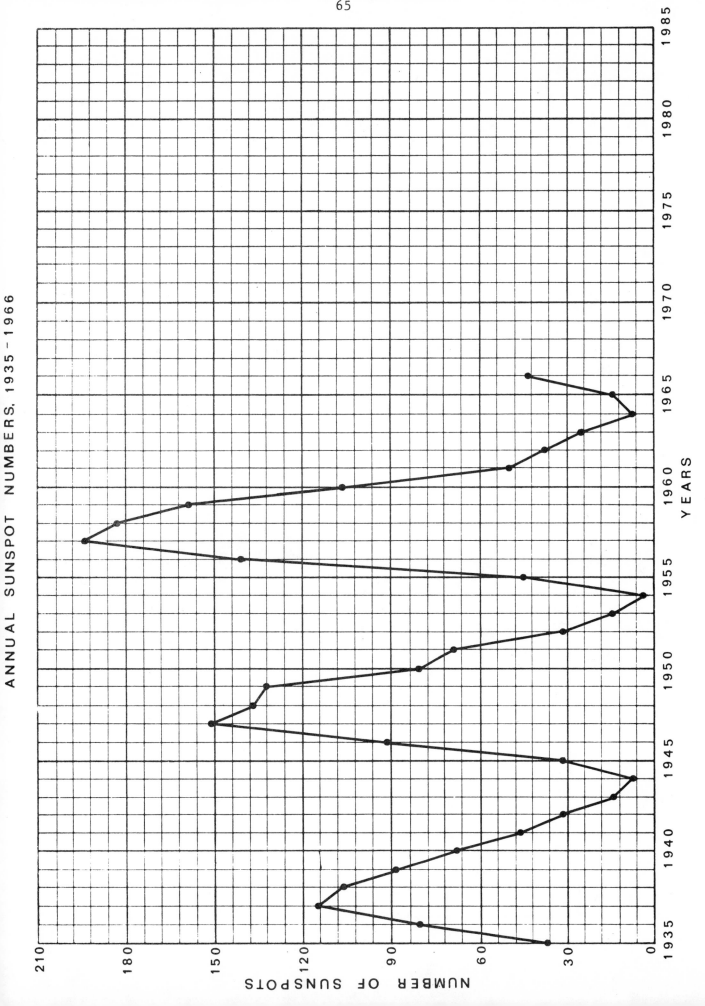

ANNUAL SUNSPOT NUMBERS, 1935-1966

Further, if you were thinking about buying a C.B. radio for use between the years 1978 and 1980, would this be a wise move in terms of what we anticipate about sunspot activity? Why?

A wise move? Why?

If you don't think that it would be wise to purchase a C.B. radio between 1978 and 1980, when do you think you could purchase one and get maximum benefit out of it?

When to buy? Your data?

Educationally, there ought to be a concept that can be gained from the sunspot data you have been inspecting. If you were to develop a "rule" or "generalization" concerning sunspot activity for others to learn, how might you state it? Using the sunspot data at your disposal, write such a rule or generalization. Do this below.

Generalization:

Recording and
Interpreting
Ecological Data *

It is much easier to report and interpret data in science when it is reported in an orderly, organized manner. Similarly, many situations appear to demand the use of graphically presented information. Regardless of the mode used, accurate and clear communication of data in science is critically important.

A demonstration of the need for clear, concise communication seems in order. We will use historical ecological data for this purpose.

Significant fluctuations in the deer population occurred on Arizona's Kaibab Plateau between 1905 and 1938. These population figures represent one of the classic case studies in North American wildlife management. In 1907 there were approximately 6,000 deer on the plateau. By 1910 they had increased in number to 10,000 and by 1915 the population had risen to 25,000. The year 1920 saw approximately 56,000 deer present and by 1923 the population had soared to 100,000. 1925 saw the population decrease to 85,000 and by 1930 it had fallen to 30,000. In 1935 there were but 14,000 deer present and in 1938 the population had been reduced to 9,000 animals.

Now let's present these same data in a different format. They follow:

Deer Populations on the Kaibab Plateau from 1907 to 1938

Year	Approx. Population of Deer
1907	6,000
1910	10,000
1915	25,000
1920	56,000
1923	100,000
1925	85,000
1930	30,000
1935	14,000
1938	9,000

If you had to comprehend and interpret the Kaibab deer population figures, which of the above two presentations would you prefer using? Certainly, it is obvious that the tabular presentation far surpases the written paragraph presentation. However, is there still a better way - or, an equally effective means of communicating these data?

We are going to ask you to graph these same data using the graph paper found on the following page. A line graph would probably be the most efficient. Please do this graph at this point in time.

* - Adapted from H. R. Hungerford and R. A. Litherland. Process Modules for Investigating Environmental Problems. Published by the authors, 1975.

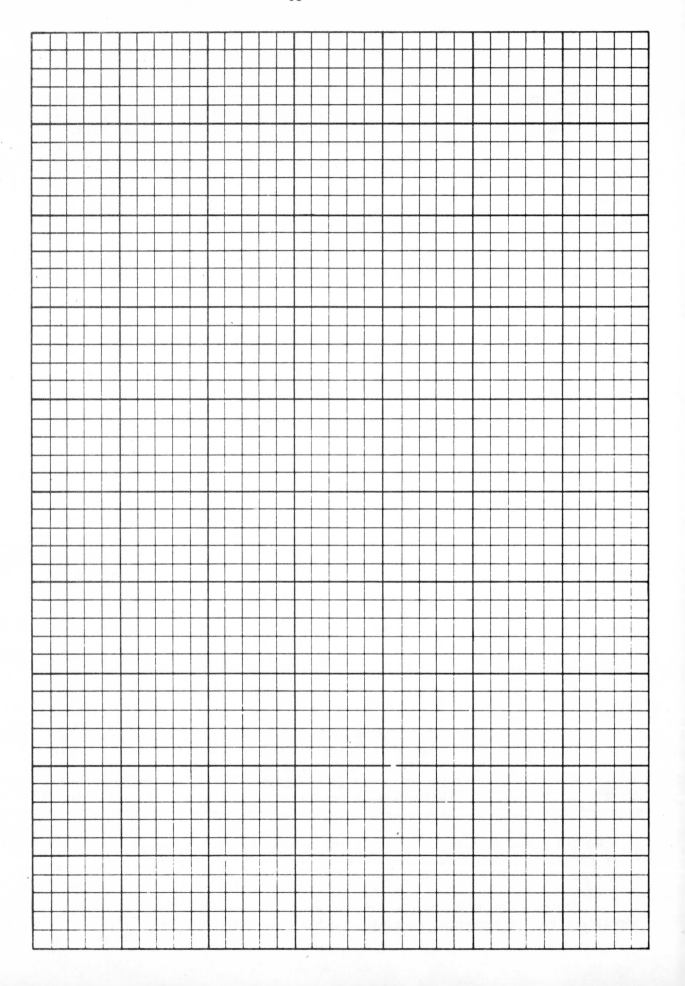

You now have available three separate models of the Kaibab deer population data. Which would you prefer to use for interpreting data? What are the implications here for children working in science in elementary school classrooms?

In keeping with the intent of this activity, we are going to ask you to use these data for the application of several science process skills. First, what conclusion can you produce from the deer population data? In science, the conclusion is a term that is often abused. A conclusion is a statement of an observation. It is not an inference. With this definition in mind, produce a defensible conclusion from the data. The conclusion should adequately reflect all the data.

Conclusion:

What logical, scientific inference can be stated concerning these data? If you recall than an inference is an expression of an explanation of an observation, you will quickly realize that any inference stated on the data at this point would, by necessity, have to be quite vague and largely meaningless. Once again, this points up the need for knowledge in conducting the business of science.

With additional information, you should be able to infer at a high level of competence. Let's see how well you can infer with more information given.

Between 1907 and 1923, 300 coyotes and 600 mountain lions were killed on the Kaibab Plateau. For the years between 1907 and 1923, write the best possible inference you can from all the data available.

Inference:

More information might make your Kaibab inference even more powerful. Once again, we will provide additional information. During the years of increasing and decreasing deer populations, the range of the deer was so badly overgrazed that thousands upon thousands of deer died from starvation. What logical inference can you now pose based on all available data (1907-1938)?

My best inference:

The "All Purpose" Process Model[*]

This process model incorporates several of the process in which you have already received training plus a few new ones. These processes include observation, comparison, hypothesizing, controlling variables, data collection, graphing, data interpretation, and experimentation.

Hopefully, upon completion of this model you will understand how many science processes or critical thinking skills can be used in combination during a problem-solving situation. Also, it is hoped that the relationship between process and product in science will be better understood.

In this model you will work with the pendulum. To make a pendulum system you will need some sort of support structure (one will probably be provided). From this support structure a string is suspended. At the bottom of the string you will need to affix some sort of weight holder like a shower curtain hook which will hold metal washers or a paper cup which can hold sand or marbles. The figures which follow in this model should help you perceive how a pendulum is set up.

Some of the variables or factors operating in this process model with which you need to become familiar are:

1. The <u>length</u> of the pendulum is the distance from the place the string is affixed to the structure to the bottom of the weight holder. See diagram below:

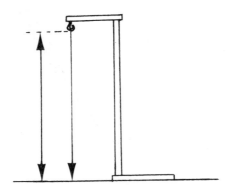

----

   [*] - Parts of this model were written by William J. Bluhm and adapted from Unit 1, Motion, in the fifth grade level of <u>Elementary Science Learning by Investigation</u> (ESLI), Rand McNally & Co., Chicago, 1974.

2. <u>Weight</u> in the pendulum system can be measured
    <u>by</u>:   (1) the actual weight of the objects
    suspended in the system, i.e., the actual
    weight of the sand, the marbles, or the washers,
    or, (2) the total <u>number</u> of objects being
    suspended in the system, i.e., 2 marbles =
    2 marble units; 5 washers = 5 washer units.

3. <u>Displacement</u> in the pendulum system is the
    length the pendulum is moved from its
    <u>stationary</u> <u>position</u>.   In the diagram below,
    the displacement is equal to 40 cm.

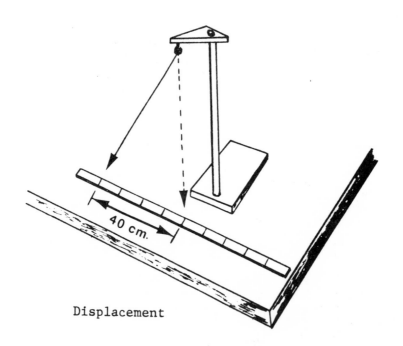

Displacement

4. <u>Vibration</u> in the pendulum system is a <u>complete</u> <u>swing</u>
forward and back from the point at which the pendulum
was displaced. Please refer to the following diagram.

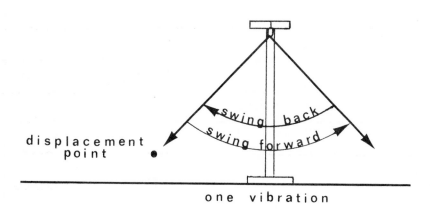

5. <u>Frequency</u> is the number of vibrations that takes
place within a specified time span.   For example,
if the time span specified is 30 seconds and the
pendulum has 10 vibrations in 30 seconds, the
<u>frequency</u> is 10 vibrations in 30 seconds.

Activity 1 -

What do you think will happen to a pendulum's <u>frequency</u> if the weight
in the pendulum system is <u>increased</u>?

In the space provided below, form a hypothesis that will describe
what you think will happen.

Hypothesis: _____

_____

_____

_____

Experiments are developed to test hypotheses which scientists feel need
to be tested. Please design and conduct an experiment to test the hypothesis
written above.

Record the data you collect in the table which can be found on the following
page.

Weight-Frequency Experiment Data

Trial	Weight	Displacement	Length	Frequency (30 Sec.)
1				
2				
3				
4				
5				
6				
7				
8				

Now, interpret your collected data in the space below:

Do the data support or refute your hypothesis? Mark your decision below:

Hypothesis decision: _____ Accept   _____ Reject

_____ Suspend Judgment and Redo Experiment

Discussion: Which variable did you manipulate or have under your control? Weight? Right! In an experiment, the manipulated variable or the variable the experimenter has control over is called the independent variable.

Which variable did you think might respond to the manipulation of weight? Frequency? Probably! In an experiment, the variable that responds to the manipulated variable is called the responding variable or the dependent variable.

During the experiment to test the relationship between increasing weight and frequency, what displacement and length did you use? Did you hold these variables constant, i.e., did you use the same displacement in each of the 6 - 8 trials and did you use the same length in each of the trials? If you didn't hold these variables constant or control the variables displacement and length, you need to redo the experiment. Why? Because, if you change the variables of weight, displacement and/or length at the same time, will you definitely know which variable the frequency is responding to - change in weight (?), change in displacement (?), or change in length (?) ?

In an experiment, only one variable should be manipulated at a time. All other variables except the responding variable should be held constant or controlled.

Activity 2 -

Hypothesize as to what you think will happen to the frequency when displacement is increased in a pendulum system.

Write your hypothesis below.

Hypothesis: _____

_____

_____

_____

Perform an experiment to test this hypothesis. Answer the following:

Which variable is the manipulated or dependent variable? _____

_____

Which variable is the responding or independent variable? _____

_____

Which variables are under control? _____

_____

Displacement-Frequency Test Data

Trial	Weight	Displacement	Length	Frequency (30 Sec.)
1				
2				
3				
4				
5				
6				
7				
8				

Data interpretation:

Hypothesis decision: _____ Accept _____ Reject

_____ Suspend Judgment and Redo Experiment

Activity 3 -

Hypothesize as to what you think will happen to the frequency when length is increased in a pendulum system.

Write your hypothesis below.

Hypothesis: _____

_____

_____

_____

Perform an experiment to test this hypothesis. Answer the following:

Which variable is the manipulated or dependent variable? _____

_____

Which variable is the responding or independent variable? _____

_____

Which variables are under control? _____

_____

Length-Frequency Test Data

Trial	Weight	Displacement	Length	Frequency (30 Sec.)
1				
2				
3				
4				
5				
6				
7				
8				

Data interpretation:

Hypothesis decision: _____ Accept _____ Reject

_____ Suspend Judgment and Redo Experiment

Next, on the following pages of graph paper, prepare three (3) graphs which illustrate the relationships between: (1) frequency and weight, (2) frequency and displacement, and (3) frequency and length. Use the data you collected in Activities 1, 2, and 3 in preparing the graphs. In each graph locate the independent variable on the horizontal axis and the dependent variable on the vertical axis.

Upon completion of the three graphs, respond to the following assignment: Interpret all graphed data. Use your data interpretation to produce a rule or principle which summarizes the influence of weight, displacement, and length in a pendulum system.

Principle:

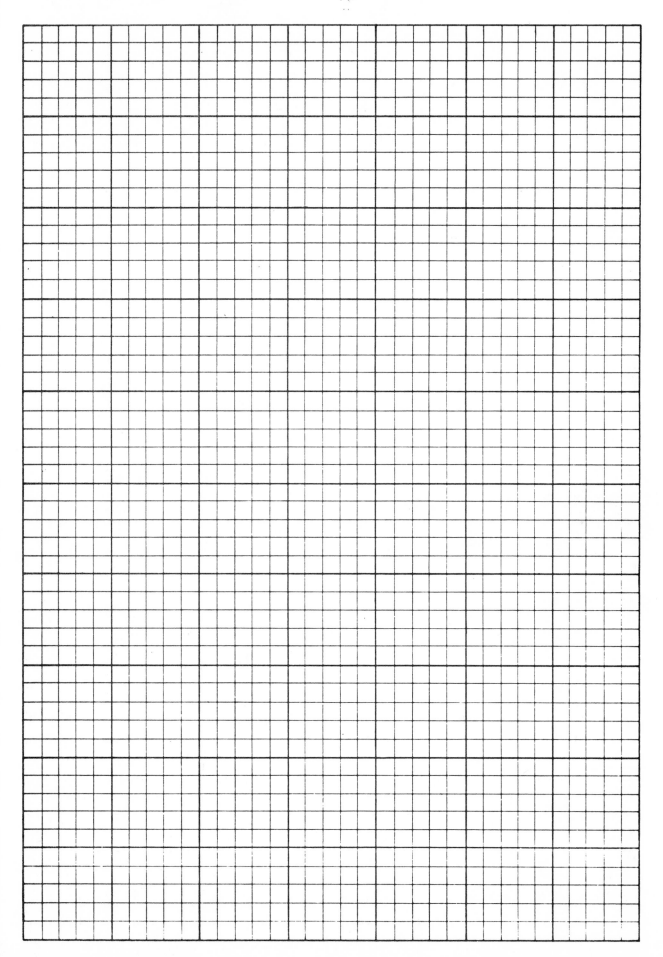

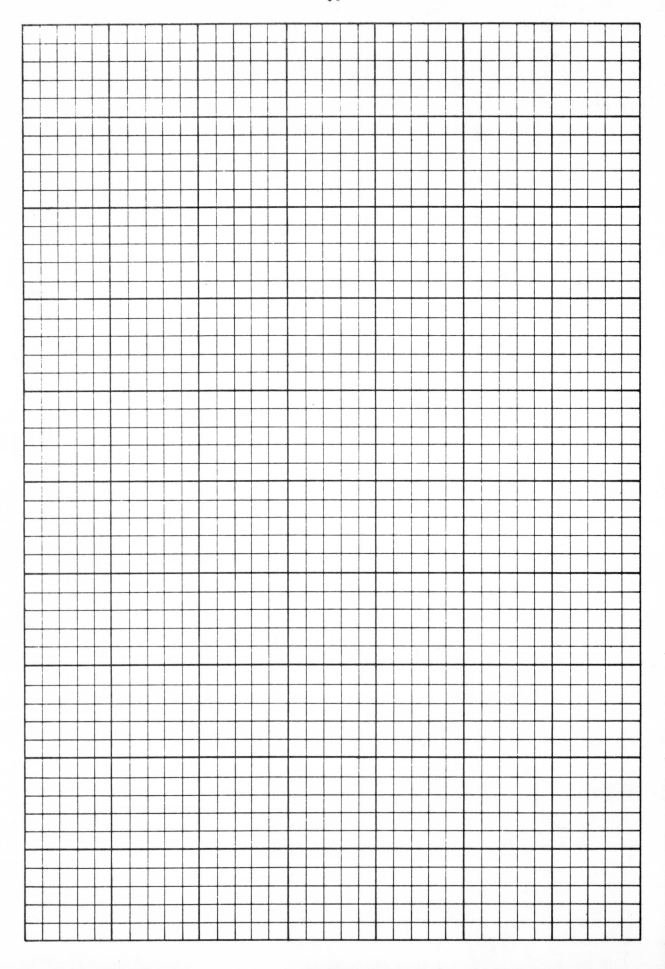

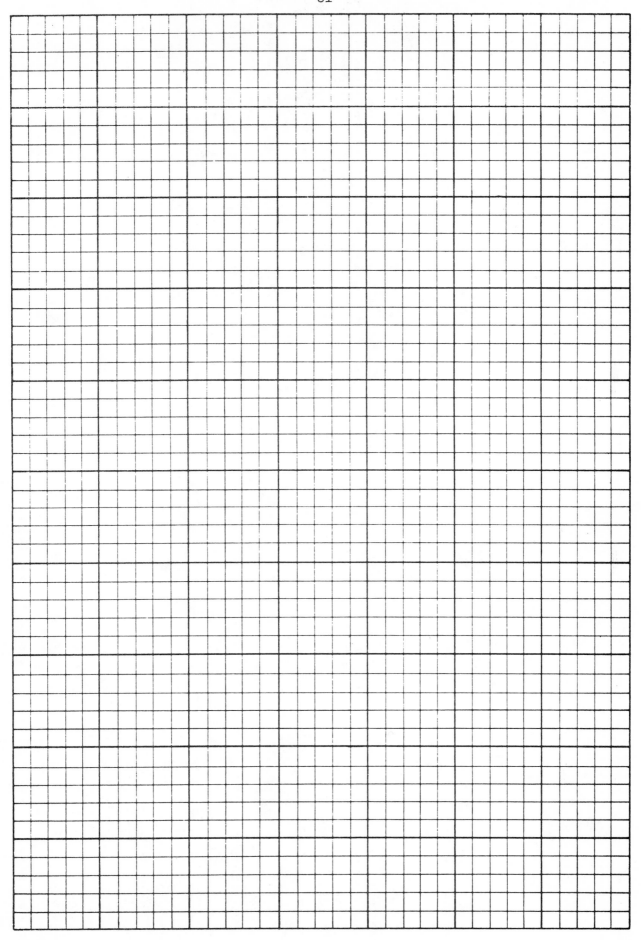

PART VI

The Affective Component: Scientific Attitudes and the Scientist

Performance Objectives

Subsequent to your interaction with Part VI you will be expected to be able to . . .

1. . . . identify man's cultural stimuli which generate erroneous concepts of scientists.

2. . . . produce and logically defend a generalized description of a "scientist" based on all the information at your disposal relative to process, product and scientific attitudes.

3. . . . explain why the "scientific method" often taught in textbooks can be an erroneous concept concerning how a scientist goes about the business of doing science.

4. . . . on the basis of the anecdotes regarding Copernicus, Galileo, Charles Darwin and Jane Goodall, build a logical rationale as to why empiricism and theology are not philosophically compatible adversaries.

5. . . . defend the following statements: Scientists are empiricists but not free spirits. They have a responsibility to recommend how their scientific discoveries should be used by society.

6. . . . prepare a list of scientific attitudes as discussed in this section. Construct a rationale regarding the advantage(s) of each attitude in advancing and validating the work of science.

7. . . . explain the value of chance happenings in science in light of the work done by scientists such as Wilhelm Konrad Roentgen (1845-1923) and Sir Alexander Fleming (1881-1955). Also, explain why some scientists can make important contributions by virtue of chance happenings when other scientists who have access to the same data cannot.

8. . . . defend the teaching of the characteristics of scientists and their scientific attitudes in elementary classrooms. Describe at least three methods of instruction which could be used by the classroom teacher to accomplish the development of said concepts.

9. . . . when presented with an anecdotal account of a scientific investigation, analyze the situation in terms of a) the scientific attitudes utilized by the scientist and b) the attitudes ignored or violated by him. Subsequently. on the basis of the above, evaluate the validity of the scientist's discovery.

10. . . . submit, in writing, using no more than 500 words, a biographical sketch of a scientist of your choice. Information in the report
should include: cogent biographical data, personality characteristis,
technological applications of his discovery(ies) and an identification of
the scientific attitudes he used in his work.

The Affective Component: Scientific Attitudes and the Scientist

If asked to envision a scientist in your mind's eye, what kind of an
individual would you "see"? Unfortunately, many would depict the scientist in a laboratory setting, bearded, with eyeglasses, preoccupied and
white-coated, at times completely oblivious to the world around him. From
where does one gather the stimuli with which to form such a generalization?
If you are at all like most people, such a stereotype is arrived at via
comic strips, the recent onslaught of Frankenstein-type movies, science
fiction novels and various science-oriented, animated television programs.
Yet, is this stereotype an accurate one, if in fact, an appropriate
stereotype exists?

Unless it has been your fortune (or misfortune) to personally know a
scientist or at least to study some of the biographical data concerning past
and present scientists, you are probably a captive of the former "scientist
concept". Realistic experiences such as those just mentioned might yield
distinctly different perceptions of a scientist. You might then understand
that scientists are human beings with likes and dislikes, joys, fears and
worries just like other people. He (or she) may even have a family, financial
problems, toothaches and all the other common concern of any citizen. They
are all individuals, with individual differences, so it would be most difficult
to describe an average scientist.

There are hundreds of thousands of working scientists throughout the
world. Amazingly, it is estimated that approximately 90% of all scientists
who ever lived are still living today. These scientists work in many different kinds of investigations and in many science fields. An individual
scientist may be a man or a woman from any nation, any race and any background with a personality and abilities which differ from the next scientist
you might meet.

In terms of their work, not all scientists operate scientifically in the
same manner. Some scientists have great experimental ability. Some collect
data using keen powers of observation, while a few use the data collected by
the former groups and assemble the information mentally into meaningful theories.
Each scientist may have his/her own way of attacking a scientific problem.
Therefore, the manner in which science proceeds is really quite different
from the series of steps often listed in textbooks and called the "scientific method".

Often, in order to appreciate the work of a scientist, it is important
to know something about the period in which he or she lived or is living.

Throughout history many scientists challenged widely accepted beliefs or drastically revolutionized man's thinking as a consequence of their new and unique findings. Some scientists, such as Copernicus and Galileo, were ridiculed and harrassed by their fellow citizens for they challenged prevailing knowledge which was supported by the clergy, who were the political leaders of the time. In fact, some of Galileo's discoveries verified the discovery of Copernicus concerning the movement of planetary bodies a half century after Copernicus had published his findings. Galileo supported the theory that the sun, not the earth, was the center of the universe! Demoting the earth from its position as center of the universe was most unsettling. Galileo's coservative opponents persuaded Pope Pius V to declare Copernicanism a heresy and Galileo was forced into silence in 1616. Later, Galileo was brought before the Inquisition on charges of heresy and was forced to renounce any views which supported Copernican Theory. Upon his death a few years later, his adversaries won another victory by refusing him burial in consecrated ground! It was not until verification by Isaac Newton, one hundred and fifty years later, that both Copernican and Galilean astronomical theories were finally fully accepted.

Charles Darwin challenged theological dogma with his Theory of Evolution which was supported by empirical observations collected over many years. In fact, this controversy continues today.

Louis Pasteur discovered bacterial causation for diseases and also, through his experimentation, yielded a death blow to the Theory of Spontaneous Generation. For his efforts Pasteur was shunned by his own scientific colleagues. His Germ Theory of Disease had violated on of the revered scientific precepts extant at that time!

In 1960, an English anthropologist, Jane Goodall, chose to leave the civilized environment of London and presently lives in the wilds of Africa. To many people, this might seem like an absurd thing to do. Not many women would trade a life of relative comfort and culture for a tent and lorry in the African Bush! Yet in order for Jane to do her work, which involves the study of the behavior of chimpanzees and vultures in their natural habitat, that's "where it's at!" Her observations on ape behavior have helped other scientists in their study of prehistoric man and the way he developed. Jane, like Darwin, has added much which may continue to stir the controversial pot of evolution.

Since scientists are individuals with their own personal and work idiosyncrasies, one might begin to wonder just what is a scientist? Is there anything which links people such as Galileo, Copernicus, Darwin, Pasteur and Jane Goodall? Are there some commonalities among scientists? Most scientists would agree that there are.

In essence, scientists share a particular outlook or attitude which directs their work. A scientific affect (attitude) may very well be the common denominator among scientists. This attitudinal set has many components, not all of which are totally agreed on by scientists or science educators. However, the effect of scientific attitudes is so tremendous in terms of the scientific enterprise that a discussion of science without considering scientific attitudes would be as incomplete as studying science without mentioning intellectual processes.

In the earlier stages of the development of science, most investigation stemmed from man's urge and need to seek rational answers to his many questions. It was somewhat analogous to the mountain climber who climbs mountains "because they are there". Curiosity was the affective stimulus for scientific study. The scientist still studies the objects and phenomena of the universe because he is curious and receives intellectual satisfaction in discovering and interpreting them. This dynamic search for answers provided impetus for the vehicle of investigation. Without the attitudes of curiosity and intellectual satisfaction, science would never have reached the mammoth proportions it has.

In present day science, curiosity and intellectual satisfaction are still attitudinal components. However, as our culture has developed and become more complex, scientists are sometimes stimulated to investigate facets of the universe, not just because of the former attitudes but because economic, social and political demands are brought to bear on the choice of what scientists investigate. Often, the scientist cannot be a free spirit in his choice of work but must bend to needs as perceived by society. Although this may sound contradictory to the ethic of empiricism discussed in Parts I and II, this is not the case. When the scientist is involved in working on a scientific problem, he still operates empirically. He is a seeker of scientific truth. At one time in history, the scientist could operate empirically and not be concerned that practical applications be found for the results of his investigations. He did not need to be connected to or concerned with the uses of his findings. In our present age, scientists rarely have such freedom. In fact, as a scientist-citizen, he probably has a greater responsibility to use his influence to help determine what applications are made of his work. He has a set of responsibilities to make his opinions known to other citizens and to those who directly decide on technological applications even though he may have no <u>direct</u> <u>control</u> over what uses are made of his discoveries. Once he has communicated the results of his work, and made his knowledge public, it belongs to society, yet he can and should use his influence as a scholar to recommend how findings are applied.

Inherent within an empirical attitude is a firm conviction not to believe in superstitions. Scientist have a healthy respect for empirical logic. Nothing is intuitively based. Along with this is a belief that nothing, no matter how strange and mysterious, ever happens or could happen without a cause. Scientists proceed in their work with the belief that the universe is empirically lawful and orderly. This deterministic attitude directs the scientist to collect data in an effort to identify causal factors and in turn to manipulate these factors and thus modify and control the behavior he observes. Determinism is applied to all facets of scientific investigation, from the behavior of a caterpillar in search of food to the complexity of an atomic model.

Scientists are not necessarily humble individuals. At times some are justifiably proud and others even arrogant. When working scientifically, however, they must constantly repress tendencies to be dogmatic or to accept things blindly or unquestioningly. Instead, an attitude of healthy skepticism allows them to accept no statements as facts unless they are supported by sufficient proof. They demand verification and replication of the data. Coupled with skepticism are openmindedness and suspended judgment. A scientist attempts to search all avenues in terms of a given problem; to desist from forming an opinion on a given issue until he has investigated it. Humans who pre-form an opinion tend to accept only the facts that support that opinion. In science, this would be disastrous! Even though evidence which contradicts a scientist's hypothesis may be produced, openmindedness and a desire to accept experimental verification are used by the scientist. These two attitudes must be utilized to maintain science as a dynamic enterprise bent on ever-improving the exactness and completeness of the knowledge which science generates. Yet the scientist realizes that knowledge is tentative, subject to change. Also he realizes the conclusions he comes to are not dogmatic, but based on probabilities.

A scientist must have a positive approach to failure -- for, indeed, failure does exist in science. Scientists operate on the premise that "this is not the right answer but at least it has been eliminated as a possibility. Try another alternative to the problem."

Surprisingly enough, some great scientific discoveries have been initiated as a consequence of this type of "failure". Oftentimes, unexpected results or chance happenings lead to a type of serendipity or chance dis-covery. The important portion of serendipity is being able to realize that an unexpected event may be the beginning of something important.

For example, Alexander Fleming was not the first bacteriologist to observe that when molds contaminate bacterial cultures, the bacteria may not grow very well. But all other bacteriologist were simply annoyed by the fact that their cultures were contaminated and took the potential consequences of this phenomenon no further. Only Fleming thought it worthwhile to investigate the molds, even though it had nothing to do with the problem he was studying. As a result, in 1945 he shared a Nobel prize with H. W. Florey and E. B. Chain for the discovery of penicillin and its therapeutic effect for the cure of different infectious diseases.

This case study relates well to Louis Pasteur's quote, "Chance favors the prepared mind." Perhaps another scientic attitude component? Fortune does seem to favor the experimenter who is prepared to take notice of chance results. Unfortunately not all scientists are flexible enough to perceive the sometimes beneficial consequences of chance happenings.

A scientist is persistent! He thrives on the belief that there are solutions to the problems he attempts to solve. He is also cautious to separate hypotheses from solutions. When solutions are determined, however, he is equally cautious not to overextend the solution to situations other than those under experimentation. In his attempt to solve problems, he is motivated to be precise in his collection and communication of data. No vague, willy-nilly emotional statements of what experiences and/or observations might mean can be accepted. In a sense, precision and objectivity are linked to the empiricial nature of a scientist's actions as he works. He has a high regard for facts and acts in accordance with them. A non-scientist often has the tendency to see only the facts he wishes to see and to react emotionally to contradictory evidence.

Scientist are also motivated to link the precision of their data collection with a firm attempt to quantify or mathematically communicate their data when at all possible. New mathematical techniques for reporting, analyzing and organizing data are constantly demanded by the scientist and judiciously used by him. Many scientists consider mathematics to be the handmaiden of science because of its ability to yield the probabilities regarding the validity of generated knowledge. The probability statements and laws of mathematics offer him security that his generated knowledge is not due to pure chance. It is the nonperceptive layman who myopically lives with the invalid comfort that life yields yes or no, all or none answers. Unfortunately but pragmatically, a scientist must live with a degree of uncertainty because often, there are no cut and dried, right answers.

As stated earlier, there probably is no total concensus concerning the scientific attitudes by which scientists are motivated. Nor can one generalize that all scientists apply all the discussed attitudes in their work or that the ones that they do apply are equally utilized. The type of scientific work being done as well as the personality involved determines much of a scientist's complete scientific affect.

What Does This Mean to the Teacher - To the pre or inservice teacher, the question may arise, "But what significance does a discussion of scientists and their scientific attitudes have for me and/or my students?" One reason for a discussion of scientists is to help children formulate an accurate concept of what scientists are like. Mass media has done far too "good" a job of creating the stereotype originally described in this section. Rather than continuing the creation of such a stereotype, one of the purposes of valid science education should be to instill a proper perspective concerning scientists and their work. A teacher can approach such education in many ways. In all grades, if the opportunity exists, working scientists can be invited into the classroom to speak to the students about their work and themselves. (By all means do speak with the scientist yourself beforehand to assure that you have made a wise choice of speakers). In this way, children are presented with fact rather than fiction. Similarly, they have a real model with which to associate.

If your school is located near a university or firm where scientific work is taking place, a field trip to see scientists in action can usually be arranged. Many organizations are quite willing to facilitate this.

Another approach is the use of actual biographies of scientists. Students can research not only the personalities but the discoveries of such famous scientists as Archimedes, Linnaeus, William Harvey, Pierre and Marie Curie, Linus Pauling and many others. Excellent trade books. filmstrips and films are available besides the traditional pedantic encyclopedia. Oral and

written reports can be prepared. Such historical research can also indicate
to the students (if the students are themselves aware of them) the specific
attitudes and intellectual processes the scientists used. Often the
children will discover the ways that some scientists have changed the course
of human history even though this was not the scientist's intent.

In terms of scientific attitudes, many of these are highly applicable
for non-scientists and for students for general education purposes. An
awareness and use of such attitudes as openmindedness and verification of
information should help students not only in science class but in their daily
lives.

In Summary -   A scientist is a human being who utilizes
                                 various scientific processes to make care-
                                 ful inquiries into the objects and happenings
around him/her. He is able to put his findings into an organized and meaningful
system of knowledge that can be used by other human beings. A scientist is
intelligent and able to solve problems. The two aspects which set him/her aside
from others are their unique abilities to use the skills of science and the
attitudes with which they go about the business of being scientific. Some of
the attitudes are: curiosity, empiricism, intellectual satisfaction, aversion
to superstition, determinism, skepticism, openmindedness, suspension of
judgment, willingness to change opinion, acceptance of experimental verification,
persistence, a positive approach to failure, precision, a view to capitalize on
chance results, belief in the potential solutions to scientific problems, objectivity, a high regard for facts and acceptance of mathematical probabilities to
validate knowledge. Students should be made aware of the realities of what
scientists and their attitudes are in order to help them have a valid concept
of the entire scientific enterprise.

A Problem   .   Now that several scientific attitude
Situation -   components have been discussed, try your
                                   hand at analyzing an anecdotal situation
in the following context: (1) What scientific attitudes were used by Mr. Jones?
(2) Which attitudes were ignored or violated by Mr. Jones? Read the following
passage carefully and prepare such a listing. In your opinion, how much
validity can be given to Mr. Jones' scientific discovery? Why?

THE FOGS OF AUGUST - SAGA OF CLY MAT JONES

Seldom is science blessed with a man of the brilliant and articulate
nature of Mr. Cly Mat Jones, an unsung but dedicated meteorological researcher.
Although odd to claim so much for a non PhD, one must remember that Cly Mat
Jones was mostly self-educated, his only genuine experience with graduate
education being a brief year's work at the Southern Mississippi Institute of
Climatological Studies (SMICS) on a grant from the Westerm Utah Mormon Foundation. Cly's ethical nature made him surrender the remainder of his grant
when he realized that no amount of research could prove the influence of
polygamy on God's decision that western Utah should remain arid.

Soon after leaving SMICS, Cly moved to southern Illinois where he hoped to gain admission to Graduate School in Southern Illinois University's renowned Department of Geography. This strategy was doomed to failure, however, when the Graduate School refused to accept credits earned at SMICS. Frustration threatened to consume Cly in his search for the PhD. Disheartened and out of funds, Cly took a job in a small grocery and general store in Vienna Heights, Illinois. Vienna Heights proved kind to our hero as the local citizenry soon grew to respect Cly's bright mind and appealing but diarrheic verbal behavior.

August of 1970 proved to be somewhat discrepant which stimulated Cly's renewed interest in meteorology. Trade at the general store was not always time consuming and many an hour was spent chatting with the local retired and unemployed populace. This particular August started out to be foggy in the evening hours and this phenomenon prompted several "old timers" to comment that it would surely be a snowy winter if the fogs kept up throughout the month. Cly smiled to himself when he was told that the number of August fogs would accurately predict the number of snows the following winter.

Cly had little better to do, so he began recording the dates on which fogs were observed in and around Vienna Heights. Further, his curious mind stimulated him to record whether the fogs were light valley fogs or heavy ones which extended over hill and dale.

Winter followed fall and Cly decided to keep a meteorological chart of the snowfall in and around Vienna Heights. As midwinter approached, Cly was astounded to find that, indeed, there was a correlation between his foggy and snowy data. In addition it appeared as though there was, in fact, a relation-ship between the amount of snowfall and the intensity of the fog as one went back and checked corresponding fogs and snowfalls. By spring, there was no doubt in Cly's mind - there was a relationship between the fogs of August and snowfall the following winter. The incidence of fogs and snowfall had a .97 correlation and the intensity correlation was .76. Both correlations were statistically significant. Cly had definitely shown a cause and effect relation-ship between the fogs of August and subsequent snowfalls!

Cly knew a good scientific finding when he saw one. He carefully prepared a paper on his findings and submitted it to the Royal Canadian Society on Climatological Phenomena. It never appeared in the Society's journal, however, because the editor was afraid that the Society's members would scoff at Cly - and the Society. Undaunted, Cly took his manuscript and went on a hitchhiking tour of the Midwestern U. S. geography departments only to be rebuffed at every door. Cly remembered Darwin, Galileo, and Pasteur and remained faithful to his own genius. Even the Vienna Heights Senior Chamber of Commerce voted to submit Cly's name as a candidate for a Nobel Prize, but they couldn't find the address.

So - Cly's genius remains unsung, probably because he was a man ahead of his times. Cly rests quietly now in the Vienna Heights Cemetery - the victim of a mysterious accident in 1972 - in a fog - in August.

PART VII

Models for Action - - Modern Science Programs

Performance Objectives

Subsequent to your interaction with Part VII you will be expected to be able to . . .

1. . . . identify and discuss the distinctive features of SAPA, SAPA II, ESS, AND SCIS as specified by your reading assignments and your instructor. Similarly, you will be able to identify and discuss these programs' physical and educational characteristics (as well as any limitations) as specified by your instructor.

2. . . . define the meaning of the term "process" as specified by your SAPA reading assignment.

3. . . . define the characteristics of the SAPA behavioral hierarchy and be able to trace any one lesson through the Hierarchy Chart published for Parts A, B, C, and D.

4. . . . explain and defend the following statement from an educational perspective:

> "One of the goals of SAPA is to provide the child with knowledge
> that is generalizable to new situations."

5. . . . identify the terminal goals for students who have participated in SAPA as specified in Part VII.

6. . . . state specifically how SAPA demonstrates outstanding internal consistency educationally, i.e., what are the components of the program that yield educational integrity (and what are the characteristics of these components, namely: 1. objectives, 2. curricular design, 3. instructional design, and 4. evaluation procedures).

7. . . . state specifically how the competency measure in Predicting 4 - The Suffocating Candle relates to the training the students receive in the laboratory. In other words, how is the competency measure consistent with the educational experiences of the children?

8. . . . define and differentiate between the terms extrapolation and interpolation and relate these to the process of prediction. Also, be able to define or explain the term experimental error.

9. . . . demonstrate (in class) a competency with the behaviors expected of

91

students while experiencing <u>Predicting</u> <u>4</u> - The <u>Suffocating</u> <u>Candle</u>.

10. . . . describe how ESS provides for flexibility in terms of its unit approach, its multiple grade level application of units, and its open-ended nature.

11. . . . explain why the ESS teacher must be highly competent with both instructional and evaluation methods. Similarly, explain why the ESS teacher must be one who is able to cope with a relatively unstructured learning environment.

12. . . . describe how much of the ESS program is consistent with the generalized philosophy of the "open classroom".

13. . . . state correctly the overall objective of SCIS as specified by your readings. Include in this objective the scientific literacy component as well as noting the reference to knowledge, skills, and attitudes.

14. . . . describe how the content of SCIS reflects a conceptual hierarchy and successfully compare this hierarchy with that of SAPA.

15. . . . cite evidence to support the contention that the entire SCIS program relates to an overall concept of "interaction".

16. . . . defend the position that the knowledge component of SCIS has great merit from a general education perspective.

17. . . . accurately compare SAPA, SAPA II, ESS, and SCIS (and other strategies described by this methods course, including the classic textbook approach) in at least all of the following dimensions:

  a. specific intent of the programs.
  b. scope of the programs including grade levels.
  c. sequence of event in the programs.
  d. numbers of units (lessons) taught in the programs.
  e. how objectives are communicated to teachers and students.
  f. evaluation techniques used.
  g. how much reading is required of students.
  h. experiential nature of the programs.
  i. materials provided by publisher for the teacher.
  j. whether inservice (or preservice) teacher training is necessary.

18. . . . defend the position that, although the SAPA, SAPA II, ESS, and SCIS programs differ considerably, all reflect an inductive approach to learning.

Models for Action - - Modern Science Programs

Introduction -   Although tens of thousands of elementary
                                   school children still experience either
no science at all in their classrooms or "read about science" programs,
numerous experientially based, sophisticated science programs exist. These
modern science programs have been developed over the past two decades by a
variety of agencies operating with substantial grants of money from both
private and federal sources.

Although these science programs reflect somewhat differing educational
philosophies, they have some significant common attributes. All are inquiry
oriented, i.e., children DO science and INDUCTIVELY generate knowledge. All
permit a wide range of students to experience success in science. All de-
emphasize the traditional relationship between reading ability and achievement, i.e., students experience almost no reading at all or a minimal amount.
All have been trial tested by using them with children. Further, trial testing
in schools across the nation resulted in necessary revisions of materials
before being commercially produced.

All of the modern programs demand special training for teachers in order
to be maximally effective. Although many educators seem to constantly search
for panaceas or their own private instructional Valhallas, these are not
likely to be found in modern science programs. Any program is only as good
as the teacher using it! The modern programs demand, besides training,
dedication and hard work on the part of the classroom teacher. They also
demand the support of the administration and the community. The school
board must be willing to financially support the acquisition and implementation
of the program.

Even though significant problems can arise in the implementation of
modern science programs, they are highly recommended. For the first time,
teachers have available science materials which substantially narrow the
gap between what is offered the students and their ability to function
intellectually. These programs have the ability to help transform educational
lip service concerning scientific literacy into action and the subsequent
reality of intellectually competent human beings.

In this section we will deal with three of the most popular but divergent modern programs. Sufficient background information and experiences will
be provided to permit the acquisition of functional concepts concerning each.
These experiences do not guarantee that you will become expert in any one of
these programs. However, you will acquire realistic and functional perspectives concerning these programs from both teacher and student standpoints.

SCIENCE: A PROCESS APPROACH (AAAS)

Science: A Process Approach (SAPA), or the AAAS Program, as it is sometimes called, is a K-6 science program developed by the Commission on Science Education of the American Association for the Advancement of Science. The program was designed by both scientist and educators working cooperatively over a six year period. It is commercially handled by the Ginn-Xerox Corporation.

A thorough description of the program is contained in AAAS Miscellaneous Publication 67-12 entitled Science - A Process Approach - Purposes - Accomplishments - Expectations. The following represents the substantive structure of that publication and is reprinted here with the permission of the AAAS Commission on Science Education, 1973.

Science - A Process Approach - Purposes - Accomplishments - Expectations

The development of an elementary science curriculum called Science — A Process Approach is now approaching completion. This curriculum, for children in kindergarten and grades one through six, has been developed by the commission on Science Education of the American Association for the Advancement of Science. The six-year effort has been financially supported by the National Science Foundation, and has involved the enthusiastic participation of more than a hundred scientists and educators, representing a wide spectrum of backgrounds, interests, and specialized knowledge.

Initial plans for the design of this new curriculum were formulated in two conferences held in the summer of 1962. On the basis of these conferences, the Commission on Science Education outlined a projected elementary science program which would emphasize the laboratory method of instruction and would focus upon ways of developing basic skills in the processes of science. The processes include observing, classifying, measuring, predicting, and other skills needed for scientific investigations. The annual cycle of activities which has been repeated each year has followed this sequence: (1) planning for development, during winter and spring; (2) a "summer writing conference" of scientists and teachers; (3) a fall period of revision, editing, and publication of experimental materials; (4) a simultaneous activity, beginning in the fall and extending to the next summer, of trying out the newly developed materials in a group of participating schools in various parts of the country.

Since 1964, a Newsletter describing important events and outcomes of this developmental cycle has been published (see References: AAAS Commission on Science Education, 1964-68). A summary of the program's history is given in the Newsletter, Volume 3, No. 2 (1967). Additional accounts of early events are given by Mayor (1962) and by Livermore (1964).

Characteristics of the Program

Science — A Process Approach shares certain purposes and characteristics with other modern science curricula. Like them, it is designed to present instruction which is intellectually stimulating and scientifically authentic. Like other programs, it is based upon the belief that an understanding of the scientific approach to gaining knowledge of man's world has a fundamental importance as a part of the general education of any child.

The program also has characteristics which make it different from other curricula in elementary science. The noteworthy and distinctive features of *Science — A Process Approach* may be summarized as follows:

1. Instructional materials are contained in booklets written for, and used by, the teacher. Accompanying kits of materials are designed for use by teacher and children. Except for certain data sheets in the later grades, there are no printed materials addressed to the pupil. What the teacher does is to organize and set up science problem situations designed for participation by the children.

2. The topics covered in the exercises sample widely from the various fields of science. The exercises are ordered in sequences of instruction to provide a developmental progression of increasing competence in the processes of science.

3. Each exercise is designed to achieve some clearly stated objectives. These are phrased in terms of the kinds of pupil behavior which can be observed as outcomes of learning upon completion of the exercise.

4. The coverage of fields of science is broad. Mathematics topics are included, to be used when needed as preparation for other science activities. Some of the exercises draw from the social and behavioral sciences. Most involve principles in physics, biology, and chemistry, with a lesser representation of earth sciences and astronomy.

5. What is to be learned by the children is an accumulative and continually increasing degree of understanding of, and capability in, the processes of science. Progress begins in the kindergarten with observation and description of object properties and motion, and advances through the sixth grade to the design and conduct of scientific experiments on a variety of topics.

6. Methods for evaluating pupils' achievement and progress are an integral part of the instructional program. The exercises contain tests of pupil achievement reflecting the objectives of the exercises and providing means of assessing outcomes. In addition, separate measures have been developed for use in determining pupil attainments in process skills prior to instruction.

7. A *Commentary for Teachers* and a *Guide for Inservice Instruction* include essential general information on the science principles and processes involved in the program, and a set of exercises providing opportunities for teachers to practice relevant instructional techniques.

The Meaning of Process

There are a number of ways of conceiving of the meaning of "process" as exemplified in *Science — A Process Approach*. First, perhaps, it should be mentioned that an emphasis on process implies a corresponding de-emphasis on specific science "content." Of course, the content is there — the children examine and make explorations of solid objects, liquids, gases, plants, animals, rocks, and even moon photographs. But, with some few notable exceptions, they are not asked to learn and remember particular facts or principles about these objects and phenomena. Rather, they are expected to learn such things as how to observe solid objects and their motions, how to classify liquids, how to infer internal mechanisms in plants, how to make and verify hypotheses about animal behavior, and how to perform experiments on the actions of gases. For example, in an exercise on the movement of liquids in materials (Part E), the children learn to design and carry out experiments on the relation between kinds of materials and rate of movement of liquids within them, including the control and manipulation of relevant variables; but they are not required to learn particular facts about the rate of liquid movement in blotting paper, fabrics, sand, clay, or other materials employed in the exercise. Such facts may be incidentally learned, and may be useful to the child, but the primary objective is one of learning to carry out the process of controlling variables in an experiment.

A second meaning of process, referred to by Gagné (1966), centers upon the idea that what is taught to children should resemble what scientists do — the "processes" that they carry out in their own scientific activities. Scientists do observe, and classify, and measure, and infer, and make hypotheses, and perform experiments. How have they come to be able to do these things? Presumably, they have learned to do them, over a period of many years, by practicing doing them. If scientists have learned to gain information in these ways, surely the elementary forms of what they do can begin to be learned in the early grades. This line of reasoning does not imply the purpose of making everyone a scientist. Instead, it puts forward the idea that understanding science depends upon being able to look upon and deal with the world in the ways that the scientist does.

The third and perhaps most widely important meaning of process introduces the consideration of human intellectual development. From this point of view, processes are in a broad sense "ways of processing information." Such processing grows more complex as the individual develops from early childhood onward. The individual capabilities that are developed may reasonably be called "intellectual skills," a phrase which many would prefer to the term "processes."

When one considers processes as intellectual skills, certain general characteristics become apparent. One of the most important is the degree of generalizability one can expect in human capabilities of this sort. The typical development of intellectual skills, as Piaget's work (cf. Flavell, 1963) amply reminds us, is from the very concrete and specific to the increasingly abstract and general. Highly general intellectual skills are typically formed over a period of years, and

are thought to depend upon the accumulated effects of learning a considerable variety of relatively concrete principles. Accordingly, the skills which *Science — A Process Approach* is designed to establish begin in highly specific and concrete forms, and increasing generality of these skills is systematically provided for by a planned progression of exercises. Evidence shows that these skills do generalize to a variety of new situations (*Newsletter,* 1967, Volume 3, No. 3; *An Evaluation Model and Its Application,* 2nd Report, 1968). The instructional program of *Science — A Process Approach* attempts to deal realistically with the development of intellectual skills, in the sense that the goals to be achieved by any single exercise are modest. In a longer-term sense, substantial and general intellectual development is expected to result from the cumulative effects of an orderly progression of learning activities.

Processes and Intellectual Development

There is, then, a progressive intellectual development within each process category. As this development proceeds, it comes to be increasingly interrelated with corresponding development of other processes; inferring, for example, partakes of prior development of skills in observing, classifying, and measuring. The interrelated nature of the development is explicitly recognized in the kinds of activities undertaken in grades four through six, sometimes referred to as "integrated processes," including controlling variables, defining operationally, formulating hypotheses, interpreting data, and as an ultimate form of such integration, experimenting.

A brief description of the expected sequence of development in both basic and integrated process categories is as follows. More complete descriptions of these processes are contained in the *Commentary for Teachers* (1968).

Observing. Beginning with identifying objects and object-properties, this sequence proceeds to the identification of changes in various physical systems, the making of controlled observations, and the ordering of a series of observations.

Classifying. Development begins with simple classifications of various physical and biological systems and progresses through multi-stage classifications, their coding and tabulation.

Using Numbers. This sequence begins with identifying sets and their members, and progresses through ordering, counting, adding, multiplying, dividing, finding averages, using decimals, and powers of ten. Exercises in number-using are introduced before they are needed to support exercises in the other processes.

Measuring. Beginning with the identification and ordering of lengths, development in this process proceeds with the demonstration of rules for measurement of length, area, volume, weight, temperature, force, speed, and a number of derived measures applicable to specific physical and biological systems.

Using space-time relationships. This sequence begins with the identification of shapes, movement, and direction. It continues with the learning of rules applicable to straight and curved paths, directions at an angle, changes in position, and determinations of linear and angular speeds.

Communicating. Development in this category begins with bar graph descriptions of simple phenomena, and proceeds through describing a variety of physical objects and systems, and the changes in them, to the construction of graphs and diagrams for observed results of experiments.

Predicting. For this process, the developmental sequence progresses from interpolation and extrapolation in graphically presented data to the formulation of methods for testing predictions.

Inferring. Initially, the idea is developed that inferences differ from observations. As development proceeds, inferences are constructed for observations of physical and biological phenomena, and situations are constructed to test inferences drawn from hypotheses.

Defining operationally. Beginning with the distinction between definitions which are operational and those which are not, this developmental sequence proceeds to the point where the child constructs operational definitions in problems that are new to him.

Formulating hypotheses. At the start of this sequence, the child distinguishes hypotheses from inferences, observations, and predictions. Development is continued to the stage of constructing hypotheses and demonstrating tests of hypotheses.

Interpreting data. This sequence begins with descriptions of graphic data and inferences based upon them, and progresses to constructing equations to represent data, relating data to statements of hypotheses, and making generalizations supported by experimental findings.

Controlling variables. The developmental sequence for this "integrated" process begins with identification of manipulated and responding (independent and dependent) variables in a description or demonstration of an experiment. Development proceeds to the level at which the student, being given a problem, inference, or hypothesis, actually conducts an experiment, identifying the variables, and describing how variables are controlled.

Experimenting. This is the capstone of the "integrated" processes. It is developed through a continuation of the sequence for controlling variables, and includes the interpretation of accounts of scientific experiments, as well as the activities of stating problems, constructing hypotheses, and carrying out experimental procedures.

Description of Intellectual Development

Descriptions of these sequences of intellectual development serve a number of purposes in the execution of the educational program embodied in *Science — A Process Approach.* These descriptions are contained in behavioral hierarchies, which bear a derivative relation to the learning hierarchies described by Gagné (1965) for smaller portions of various curricula. A chart depicting the behavioral hierarchies for all of the simpler processes has recently been published (Process Hierarchy Chart, 1967), and an explanation of them is also given in booklets introducing each Part, entitled *Description of the Program*.

The behavioral hierarchies constitute the "skeleton" of *Science — A Process Approach* and the rationale for selecting and ordering the sequence of exercises. Thus the behavioral hierarchies orient the teacher to the purposes of the program, or of any portion of it. The teacher may examine the progression of behavioral development depicted in these hierarchies, and derive from them a view of where teaching starts and where it is expected to go. In addition, they show the interrelationships between any one exercise and others which precede or follow it, including those primarily devoted to other processes. To aid the teacher in maintaining this viewpoint towards the progressive development of processes, there is included in each exercise a section showing the relevant preceding steps and subsequent steps in the behavioral hierarchy. This section is, in actuality, simply a small portion of the entire hierarchy, providing the teacher with a rather specific view of what has gone before and what is coming next. The interpretation of such diagrams is expected to be: (1) here are the prerequisites for the present exercise; (2) here is what the child is expected to learn in this exercise; and (3) this is what the exercise will prepare him to undertake in later learning.

The second major use of the behavioral hierarchies is as guides to the assessment of student achievement and program evaluation (*Newsletter*, 1967, Volume 3, No. 3; Walbesser, 1963). Initial evaluation of the student, to determine whether or not he has achieved the objectives of each exercise, is carried out by performance tests based upon the objectives stated in the exercises themselves. Such tests, however, are designed to be consistent with the behavioral hierarchies, so that in each case what is being measured is a new achievement, and not something that has already been achieved as a result of some earlier exercise.

In addition, provision must be made to measure achievement in a sense other than as the immediate effects of instruction; in fact,

in a developmental sense. The basis for such measurement is again the developmental sequence of the behavioral hierarchy, represented in a test which attempts to assess how far a pupil has progressed in each process (*Science — A Process Approach, The Process Instrument*, 1970.) Finally, the hierarchies also guide the development of measures of achievement which are "terminal" to the program, insofar as they help to define what the minimum set of behaviors may be for children who have participated in the program for a period of years.

Purposes of the Program

The major characteristics of *Science — A Process Approach* which have been described surely serve in large part to convey what the program is all about. Some additional understanding of the approach, however, may be gained from an account of the purposes which have guided the effort. An important statement of these purposes was prepared at an early stage of development by a committee of the Commission on Science Education (*Science — A Process Approach, Commentary for Teachers*, 1970). In addition, several papers dealing with the goals of various aspects of the development were prepared at different points along the way and are collected together under the title *The Psychological Bases of Science — A Process Approach* (1965).

General education. From the outset, it has been a guiding purpose to develop a curriculum which could become part of the general education of every child. The goal has not been to produce students of science who have a large amount of highly specialized knowledge. Rather, the aim is for every child to acquire the basic knowledge and point of view which provide him with a highly generalized method of gaining an understanding of himself and the world in which he lives.

Preparation for systematic study of scientific disciplines. Another important guiding purpose has been to provide the student in the elementary grades with some highly generalizable intellectual skills, and some knowledge of scientific procedures for gaining new knowledge, which can serve as a springboard for later study of any of the sciences. There are some very basic ideas, it is believed, which are important to the understanding of systematic science, and which cannot be readily identified as portions of the traditional elementary curriculum. It is these ideas that are intended to be represented as the "processes" of the new science curriculum.

Generalizability of knowledge. A related aim is that of providing the child with the kind of knowledge that is generalizable to new situations. In part, this is accomplished by the use of a variety of content. In part, it is attempted by asking the child to practice making generalizations from one field of science to another. Controlling variables in an experiment on rusting of iron may be followed by an exercise that poses a problem of controlling variables in plant growth.

Level of achievement. Certainly, the program aims for a level of achievement in understanding science and making scientific investigations which has not heretofore been attained by elementary school students. The purpose is to give these children capabilities for thinking and acting in the realm of science which go far beyond what has previously been customary. It is hoped that such capabilities may be applied in all their pursuits, not solely to the further study of scientific subjects.

Intellectual challenge. The materials of the program were prepared with the aim of presenting children with intellectual challenges. Pupils are required to remember few "facts," and those few will most probably be retained without effort. However, they are frequently asked to think, to use reasoning, and to invent methods and explanations. This is considered to be an important part of what is meant by learning to use science "processes."

Pupil interest. The well-known principle of proceeding in instruction from the familiar to the unfamiliar is used throughout the program. The attempt is made to appeal to initial pupil interest, and to maintain it as new problems are introduced. Thus one important goal of instruction is to bring about a broadening of pupil interest in the many fields of science.

It is hoped that the child will come to recognize many new problems, previously unknown to him, which can be viewed scientifically; and that over the course of the program he will develop a lasting interest in science, whether or not he chooses it for a life work.

Achievement motivation. Besides the motivation of curiosity and intellectual challenge, the program intends to make use of achievement motivation. Comments from teachers and the measured achievements of children during the tryout period have been used as bases for revisions and adjustments in the exercises designed to accomplish this purpose. The exercises are aimed at *all* children, not solely the bright ones. The objectives are intended to be not too difficult for the vast majority of children to achieve. When they are achieved, this accomplishment will, it is hoped, reward the child and thus contribute to the maintenance of his interest in further exploration of science and its processes.

Accomplishments

The goals of *Science — A Process Approach*, although moderately ambitious, appear to be attainable. What evidences are there, at the present time, that progress is being made toward these goals? What accomplishments can be described?

A systematic course of study. The instructional materials of *Science — A Process Approach* (Parts A-C, 1967; Parts D and E, 1966; Parts F and G, 1970) provide the basic evidence that a systematic course of study in the processes of science has been developed. Successive exercises in each process build upon earlier exercises in a progressive sequence, while at the same time variations in subject matter are deliberately introduced.

Empirical findings concerning the existence of ordered relationships among the exercises, in the sense that successful completion of one contributes to the learning involved in a subsequent one, have been described in reports of the results of pupil testing (*Newsletter*, 1967, Volume 3, No. 3; *An Evaluation Model and Its Application*, 2nd Report, 1968). Additional findings have been obtained, and are to be reported, by administering an individual test of performance in the various processes *(The Process Instrument,* 1969) to groups of children who have participated in the program for one or more years. In general, with some notable exceptions, it has been shown that achievement of lower levels of development in each process increases the probability of attaining subsequent steps in these intellectual skills. As for the exceptions, these have led to a re-examination of the exercises and the sequencing of developmental steps; and in many instances the latter have been reordered as reflected in the most recent Process Hierarchy Chart (1967).

Continued revision for improvement. From the outset the materials of *Science — A Process Approach* have been subjected to periodic improvement based upon information collected during tryouts in 15 school systems located in various parts of the country. Reports from teachers have provided systematic information on the ease of teaching, technical difficulties, degree of pupil enthusiasm, appraisals of pupil understanding, and related matters. Measures of competence administered to children upon the completion of each exercise have yielded data on the proportion of children achieving each of the defined objectives of the exercise. The target has been to have 90% of the children achieve 90% of the objectives. Each revision of the exercises, in four successive years for each part, has been based upon these findings regarding pupil achievement and teacher reception; and each revision has approached more closely the stated goals of the program. Comprehensive accounts of the information yielded by these two sources of data have been reported *(An Evaluation Model and Its Application,* 2nd Report, 1968).

Broad coverage of science. The booklets of *Science — A Process Approach* exhibit the varied coverage of the fields of science which reflect the aims of the program. The distribution of content in relation to acepted categories of science is approximately as follows: Physical Science, 40%; Life Science, 25%, Mathematics, 18%; Earth Sciences, 10%; Social and Behavioral Sciences, 7%. An account of content coverage in biology has been de-

scribed by Kurtz (1967). Livermore (1966) has made an analysis of the content in the field of chemistry, and Mayor (1967) has given a description of the mathematics content.

Available teacher performances. Another notable accomplishment of the program has been its concerted approach to the problem of orienting and educating teachers of elementary science. The need for materials for the education of teachers was recognized early, and much effort has been devoted to the preparation of a course and accompanying materials for the teacher who is preparing to teach the program. Emphasis is given in teacher education to the science processes and their relation to human intellectual development, in addition to helping teachers acquire the competencies included in *Science — A Process Approach* for application in the classroom. The *Commentary for Teachers* is actually much more than a commentary, for it contains carefully prepared self-instructional lessons relevant to each of the processes. The materials have been tried out and evaluated in several teacher workshops; and their latest form reflects revisions based upon systematic information collected within these sessions (to be reported later in an issue of the AAAS Commission on Science Education *Newsletter).*

Still another product of development is a guide intended for the leaders of sessions for teacher education, reflecting the science processes, their psychological bases, and the variety of science activities and teaching strategies to which they lead. The *Guide For Inservice Instruction* (1967) incorporates brief instructional films, self-instructional booklets, and tests for diagnosis and evaluation of teacher learning.

Student achievements. Reports of results on program evaluation *(An Evaluation Model and Its Application,* 1968; *Newsletter,* 1967, Volume 3, No. 3) generally provide much favorable evidence regarding student achievements. For example, it has been found that immediate achievement measures indicate 90 percent of the children to have acquired at least 70 percent of the desired competencies for 97 of 102 exercises in Parts A through D. Further, 90 percent of the children reached the 80 percent level of achievement for all but fourteen of these exercises. When children who had participated in the program for one year were compared with children at the same grade level who had participated for three years, differences favoring the latter group ranged from two to twenty percent. When achievements of a group of children from a low socio-economic background were compared with those of medium and high levels of family income, it was found that although the former group completed fewer exercises, their success on the completed exercises was as high as that of the other children.

Other evidences of the effects of the program have yet to be gathered. More information will be sought on the lasting effects of this program. Answers are needed to such questions as what children know and what they are able to accomplish at the end of the fourth grade, the fifth, and the sixth, after having completed several years of *Science— A Process Approach*. In addition, it is hoped that evidence can be obtained of increased pupil interest in science, as well as an increased degree of the children's positive valuation of scientific activities after participation in the program over a period of several years.

Expectations

What will a "graduate" of *Science — A Process Approach* be like? What will he know? What will he be able to do? These questions, of course, cannot be answered at the present time with any great degree of assurance. The evidence of what these children are like will have to come, after a period of years, from evidence of what they can accomplish in grades subsequent to the sixth. Perhaps also it will come from evidence of how they behave toward science in even later periods of their lives.

The following descriptions of what may be expected of a child who has completed the program are speculative, although stated in concrete terms. They represent goals which have given implicit guidance to the development of *Science—A Process Approach*. While the full attainment of these goals is greatly to be desired, even partial attainment would surely be viewed as a substantial indication of the program's effectiveness.

1. He will tend to apply a scientific mode of thought to a wide range of problems, including social ones, distinguishing facts from conjectures and inferences, and identifying the procedures required to obtain verification of hypotheses and suggested solutions.

2. He will be able to acquire an understanding of the structure of those particular scientific disciplines he pursues in junior and senior high school more rapidly and with less difficulty than is the case with students today.

3. In a printed account of a scientific experiment, using terms that are understood or defined, he will be able to identify the question being investigated; the variables manipulated, controlled, and measured; the hypothesis being tested; how such a test relates to the results obtained; and the conclusions which can legitimately be drawn.

4. In an oral account of a scientific experiment, given by a scientist using terms intended for laymen, he will be able to identify those elements of scientific procedure and findings mentioned in 3.

5. In an incomplete account of a scientific experiment, such as might appear in a newspaper, he will be able to infer, where necessary, the question being investigated and the elements of scientific procedure described in 3.

6. Given a problem amenable to scientific investigation, and within his understanding as to factual content, he will be able to design (and under certain conditions, carry out) one or more experiments to test hypotheses relevant to the problem.

7. He will show his appreciation of, and interest in, scientific activities by choices made in reading, entertainment, and other kinds of leisure-time pursuits.

To those who have developed the program, these predictions seem not unreasonable. They are things that should happen. If and when they do, the truly important outcomes of *Science — A Process Approach* will be known.

REFERENCES

AAAS Commission on Science Education. *Newsletter.* Vols. 1-4, 1964-1968.

AAAS Commission on Science Education. *An Evaluation Model and Its Application.* Washington D. C.: American Association for the Advancement of Science, 1965. (Misc. Publ. 65-9, out of print) 2nd Report, 1968.

AAAS Commission on Science Education. *The Psychological Bases of Science — A Process Approach.* Washington, D. C.: American Association for the Advancement of Science, 1965.

AAAS Commission on Science Education.

Science — A Process Approach. Parts A-C, 1967; Parts D and E, 1968. New York: Xerox Education Division.

Science — A Process Approach. Fourth Experimental Edition, Parts Six and Seven. Washington, D. C.: American Association for the Advancement of Science, 1967.

Science — A Process Approach. Commentary for Teachers. Washington, D. C.: American Association for the Advancement of Science, 1965. (Misc. Publ. 65-22, out of print) Revision, 1968.

Science — A Process Approach. The Process Instrument. New York: Xerox Education Division. To be published in 1969.

Science — A Process Approach. Guide for In-service Instruction, 2nd Ed. Washington, D .C.: American Association for the Advancement of Science, 1967.

Science — A Process Approach. Process Hierarchy Chart. New York: Xerox Education Division, 1967.

Flavell, J. H. *The Developmental Psychology of Jean Piaget.* Princeton, N. J.: Van Nostrand, 1963.

Gagné, R. M. *The Conditions of Learning.* New York: Holt, Rinehart, & Winston, 1965, Chapter 7.

Gagné, R. M. Elementary Science: A New Scheme of Instruction. *Science,* 1966, 151, 49-53.

Kurtz, E. B. Biology in Science — A Process Approach. *American Biology Teacher,* 1967, 29, 192-196.

Livermore, A. H. The Process Approach of the AAAS Commission on Science Education. *Journal of Research in Science Teaching,* 1964, 2, 271-282.

Livermore, A. H. AAAS Commission on Science Education Elementary Science Program. *Journal of Chemical Education,* 1966, 43, 270-272.

Mayor, J. R. AAAS Commission on Science Instruction. *Science Education News,* 1962, No. 12-62, 1-4.

References, Continued:

Walbesser, H. H. 1966. Science curriculum evaluation: observations on a position. The Science Teacher, vol. 33, no. 2 (February), p. 34-39.

Walbesser, H. H. and Heather L. Carter. 1968. Some methodological considerations of curriculum evaluation research. Educational Leadership, vol. 26, no. 1 (October), p. 53-64.

Walbesser, H. H. and Heather L. Carter. 1968. Acquisition of elementary science behavior by children of disadvantaged families. Educational Leadership, vol. 25, no. 8 (May), p. 741-48.

Walbesser, H. H. and Heather L. Carter. 1970. The effect on test results of changes in task and responses format required by altering the test administration from an individual to a group form. Journal of Research in Science Teaching, 7:1-8.

SCIENCE: A PROCESS APPROACH II (SAPA II)

In 1974, as per the original National Science Foundation contract, the original SAPA program materials became public property and Ginn-Xerox lost its copyright privileges. It was at this point in time that the Xerox Corporation released, for elementary school use, a revision of the SAPA program. It is called Science: A Process Approach II (SAPA II).

The similarities of SAPA II to SAPA are many. Both programs are still predicated on a behavioral hierarchy. Both were field tested with children. They are both oriented around behavioral objectives and the goal of each is the same, i.e., proficiency in the thirteen intellectual processes. Both are experiential and inductive programs. Equipment and teachers' manuals are supplied with both. Both use strong evaluative techniques. What, then, is/are the difference(s) between the two programs?

The main difference lies in the greater flexibility of the SAPA II program. Physical changes in the SAPA II curriculum complement increased flexibility in teaching procedures. Materials are packaged in a continuum of 105 "quasi"-ungraded modules (lessons). Modules contain a teacher instruction booklet and various combinations of laboratory hardware, worksheets, spirit duplicating masters and non-consumable student booklets. In essence, the modules being "quasi"-ungraded allows them to be used at various grade levels. There are modules which are classified as "key" or necessary clusters which are the basic prerequisite lessons for any one grade level. After teaching the "key" cluster, the teacher may select from a variety of alternative modules as suits his/her purpose. In this manner, the program developers have attempted to build in greater flexibility than that found in the original program.

A lesser difference is SAPA II's attempt to individualize the program. Latent image worksheets were created especially to help individualize some activities. These sheets, reproduced from special spirit duplicating masters, contain not only questions and space for student comments, but also responses which remain invisible until the lesson is complete and the sheet is rubbed with a special marker. The images then appear on the sheet, and students can check their own work and benefit from the immediate feedback thus provided. It is interesting to note that the above technique increases the dependency of the child on his own reading ability -- something which the original program did not necessitate.

Though some of the program components of SAPA II are different, the majority of lesson topics remain essentially the same as those used in SAPA. On the following two pages is a listing of the 105 SAPA II modules and the intellectual process covered by each.*

---

* - This listing was taken from Science . . . A Process Approach II, The Modular Science Curriculum, The Architecture of a Revision by Ginn and Company, a Xerox Education Company, Publication No. M16921.

The 105 Modules of Science . . . A Process Approach II

In graded schools, modules 1 through 12 or 1 through 15 usually constitute Kindergarten, 13 through 24 or 16 through 30 constitute Grade 1, and so on, in groups of 12 to 15 modules per year.

Module Number	Module	Process
1	Perception of Color	Observing/a
2	Recognizing and Using Shapes	Space/Time/a
3	Color, Shape, Texture, and Size	Observing/b
4	Leaves, Nuts, and Seashells	Classifying/a
5	Temperature	Observing/c
6	Direction and Movement	Space/Time/b
7	Perception of Taste	Observing/d
8	Length	Measuring/a
9	Sets and Their Members	Using Numbers/a
10	Spacing Arrangements	Space/Time/c
11	Listening to Whales	Observing/e
12	Three-Dimensional Shapes	Space/Time/d
13	Numerals, Order and Counting	Using Numbers/b
14	Animal and Familiar Things	Classifying/b
15	Perception of Odors	Observing/f
16	Living and Nonliving Things	Classifying/c
	Trees in Our Environment	
17	Change	Observing/g
18	Using the Senses	Observing/h
19	Soils	Observing/i
20	Counting Birds	Using Numbers/c
21	Weather	Observing/j
22	Same but Different	Communicating/a
23	Comparing Volumes	Measuring/b
24	Metric Lengths	Measuring/c
25	Introduction to Graphing	Communicating/b
26	Using a Balance	Measuring/d
27	Pushes and Pulls	Communicating/c
28	Molds and Green Plants	Observing/k
29	Shadows	Space/Time/e
30	Addition Through 99	Using Numbers/d
31	Life Cycles	Communicating/d
32	A Terrarium	Classifying/d
33	What's Inside	Inferring/a
34	About How Far?	Measuring/e
35	Symmetry	Space/Time/f
36	Animal Responses	Observing/l
37	Forces	Measuring/f
38	Using Graphs	Predicting/a
39	Solids, Liquids, and Gases	Measuring/g
40	How Certain Can You Be?	Inferring/b
41	Temperature and Thermometers	Measuring/h
42	Sorting Mixtures	Classifying/e
43	A Plant Part That Grows	Communicating/e
44	Surveying Opinion	Predicting/b
45	Lines, Curves and Surfaces	Space/Time/g
46	Observations and Inferences	Inferring/c
47	Scale Drawings	Communicating/f
	A Tree Diary	Communicating/g
48	The Bouncing Ball	Predicting/c
49	Drop by Drop	Measuring/i
50	The Clean-Up Campaign	Predicting/d
51	Rate of Change	Space/Time/h
52	Plants Transpire	Inferring/d

Module Number	Module	Process
53	The Suffocating Candle	Predicting/e
54	Static and Moving Objects	Measuring/j
55	Sprouting Seeds	Observing/m
	Magnetic Poles	Observing/n
56	Punch Cards	Classifying/f
57	Position and Shape	Communicating/h
58	Liquids and Tissue	Inferring/e
59	Metersticks, Money, and Decimals	Using Numbers/e
60	Relative Motion	Space/Time/i
61	Circuit Boards	Inferring/f
62	Climbing Liquids	Controlling Variables/a
63	Maze Behavior	Interpreting Data/a
64	Cells, Lamps, Switches	Defining Operationally/a
65	Minerals in Rocks	Interpreting Data/b
66	Learning and Forgetting	Controlling Variables/b
67	Identifying Materials	Interpreting Data/c
68	Field of Vision	Interpreting Data/d
69	Magnification	Defining Operationally/b
70	Conductors and Nonconductors	Formulating Hypotheses/a
71	Soap and Seeds	Controlling Variables/c
72	Heart Rate	Controlling Variables/d
73	Solutions	Formulating Hypotheses/b
74	Biotic Communities	Defining Operationally/c
75	Decimals, Graphs, and Pendulums	Interpreting Data/e
76	Limited Earth	Interpreting Data/f
77	Chemical Reactions	Controlling Variables/e
78	Levers	Formulating Hypotheses/c
79	Animal Behavior	Formulating Hypotheses/d
80	Inertia & Mass	Defining Operationally/d
81	Analysis of Mixtures	Defining Operationally/e
82	Force & Acceleration	Controlling Variables/f
83	Chances Are	Formulating Hypotheses/e
84	Angles	Interpreting Data/g
85	Contour Maps	Interpreting Data/h
86	Earth's Magnetism	Interpreting Data/i
87	Wheel Speeds	Interpreting Data/j
88	Environmental Protection	Defining Operationally/f
89	Plant Parts	Defining Operationally/g
90	Streams & Slopes	Interpreting Data/k
91	Flowers	Defining Operationally/h
92	Three Gases	Formulating Hypotheses/f
93	Temperature and Heat	Defining Operationally/i
94	Small Water Animals	Controlling Variables/g
95	Mars Photos	Interpreting Data/l
96	Pressure and Volume	Experimenting/a
97	Optical Illusions	Experimenting/b
98	Eye Power	Experimenting/c
99	Fermentation	Experimenting/d
100	Plant Nutrition	Experimenting/e
101	Mental Blocks	Experimenting/f
102	Plants in Light	Experimenting/g
103	Density	Experimenting/h
104	Viscosity	Experimenting/i
105	Membranes	Experimenting/j

Experiencing the
SAPA Strategy -

At this point in time, each methods student will be given a set of experiences which will familiarize him/her with Science: A Process Approach (SAPA). Said experiences will include the inspection of teacher booklets at two or more levels, K-6. Further, interaction will be permitted between methods students and materials kits perpared for use with SAPA. Also, instruction in the use of The Hierarchy Chart (Xerox) will be followed by detailed interaction with the process hierarchy.

Following these activities, all students will participate in one or more units from SAPA in order that they may experience the program from the child's perspective. The initial laboratory unit experience will be with a Part D (third grade) unit entitled Predicting 4 - The Suffocating Candle (P4). P4 should be located on The Hierarchy Chart and its place in the hierarchy analyzed. (The Suffocating Candle unit is used in both the SAPA and SAPA II programs.)

What follows is a set of information and work sheets appropriate for P4. All asterisked (*) materials are taken directly from the teacher's booklet and are reprinted here with the permission of the AAAS Commission on Science Education, 1973.

The P4 Laboratory

Please follow all verbal instructions carefully during the completion of the P4 laboratory. Try to analyze this unit from both a methodological standpoint and a third grader's perspective.

Objectives of P4*   At the end of this exercise the child should be able to

1. CONSTRUCT predictions based on a series of observations that reveal a pattern.

2. CONSTRUCT a revision of a prediction on the basis of additional information.

Rationale for P4*   This exercise illustrates the use of the term prediction in the context of a simple scientific inquiry. Often, the scientist reasons from past or present experience in order to predict the results of a future trial of some event from many partial data. The outcome of the event will then either confirm or refute that prediction.

There are several aspects of the process of predicting that should be recognized. For example, the outcome of an event may confirm a prediction accidentally. To help insure against this possibility, the scientist repeats his tests. Although it is possible to obtain identical results accidentally, the probability of such an occurrence is very low.

When a test is repeated and the result is different, the scientist may infer that not all the conditions in both tests were the same. He then needs to evaluate these conditions to determine whether all conditions were in fact the same, or whether some were different or he overlooked some significant condition. The nature and importance of <u>experimental</u> <u>error</u> is thus emphasized.

Even a prediction that is not borne out by a test can be valuable, and it should not be dismissed too quickly. For example, it can be useful to explore the basis for the prediction more fully. The scientist may have emphasized one piece of his observational evidence at the expense of some other important parts, or he may simply have made a mistake in his analysis. Such a prediction can also point out the need for new observational evidence.

In the activities of this exercise, the children will first observe a burning candle that is covered by a glass jar. They will then predict whether the burning time will be longer or shorter with a smaller jar. Then, on the basis of measurements of both the jar volume and the burning time, they will make more precise predictions of burning time. Finally, they will compare the validity of predictions based on interpolation with those based on extrapolation of the data on a graph.

Vocabulary for P4*

experimental error

interpolation

extrapolation

Data Collection Sheet – Predicting 4 – The Suffocating Candle

Jar	Jar Volume	Predicted Burning Time	Burning Time (Seconds)			Mean Time – $\overline{X}$
			Trial 1	Trial 2	Trial 3	
C		XXXXXXXXXXXX				

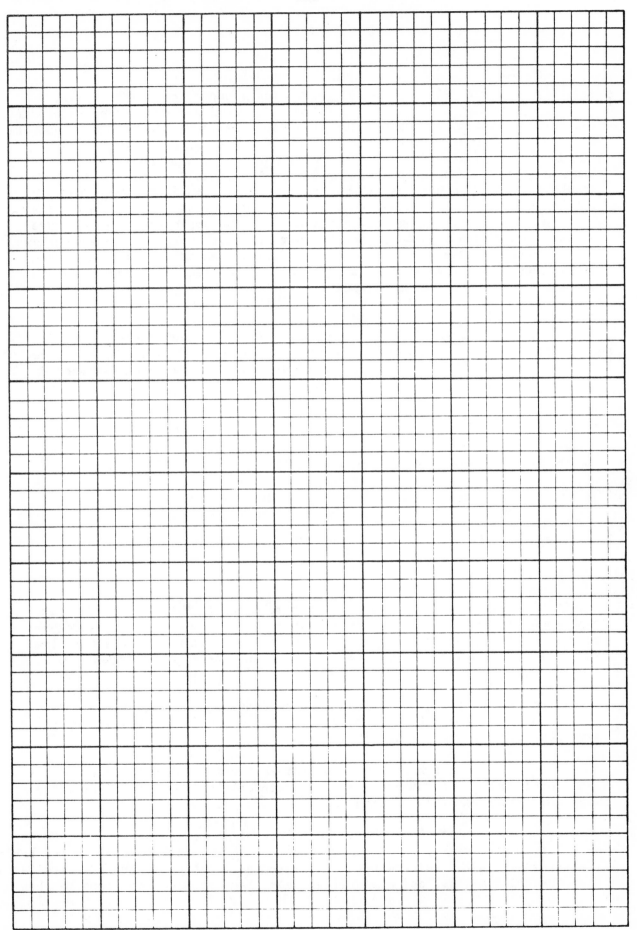

Appraisal for P4*   Give each group of children a tall,
                                    narrow jar, and ask the groups to predict
the burning time of a candle under this jar. Ask, HOW LONG WOULD YOU DO THIS?
They should suggest making the volume measurement using their arbitrary
standard, the smallest jar. Ask them to make the volume measurement of this
jar and then to predict the burning time. They should predict from their
graphs. If they do not, ask them specifically to use their graph to make
another prediction. Then ask them to carry out the test to determine the
burning time. Check to see whether they make the measurement two or more
times, rather than just once, and whether or not they report a mean burning
time. Then ask them to compare their observed mean buring times with their
predictions. Also ask whether they have interpolated or extrapolated and
how they would interpret the results.

Competency Measure   (Note: The P4 Competency Measure Work-
    for P4*   sheet found on the next page is for methods
                                    students use. It has been designed speci-
fically for this purpose by the authors.

Competency Measure

TASKS 1, 2 (OBJECTIVE 1): Give the child a sheet of paper with the following
table of data or put the data on the chalkboard.

Number of Ice Cubes	Melting Time (minutes)
4	20
8	60

Now say, I am going to describe a simple test: Two jars of the same
size and shape were half-filled with water. Four ice cubes were added to
one jar, and eight to the other. The experimenter then observed that the
four ice cubes took twenty minutes to melt, and the eight ice cubes took
sixty minutes.

Predict how long it will take six ice cubes to melt under the same
conditions. Put one check on the acceptable column for Task 1 if the child
says some time between 30 and 50 minutes.

Then say, Predict how long it will take two ice cubes to melt under the
same conditions. Put one check in the acceptable column for Task 2 if he
says something less than 20 minutes.

TASK 3 (OBJECTIVE 1): Give the child a copy of the graph shown . . . Point
out that the two marked points correspond to the two number pairs in the table.
(If necessary, use a colored pencil to make the location of the points clear.)
Give the child a ruler and a pencil and say, Make an X on the graph to show

P4 Competency Measure Worksheet

Competency Measure for Lesson: Part D – Predicting 4 – "The Suffocating Candle":

OBJECTIVES:

1. . . . to CONSTRUCT predictions based on a series of observations that reveal a pattern.

2. . . . to CONSTRUCT a revision of a prediction on the basis of additional information.

NUMBER OF ICE CUBES	MELTING TIME IN MINUTES
4	20
8	60

	TEACHER'S RECORD	
T	ACCEPTABLE RESPONSE	UNACCEPT. RESPONSE
1		
2		
3		
4		

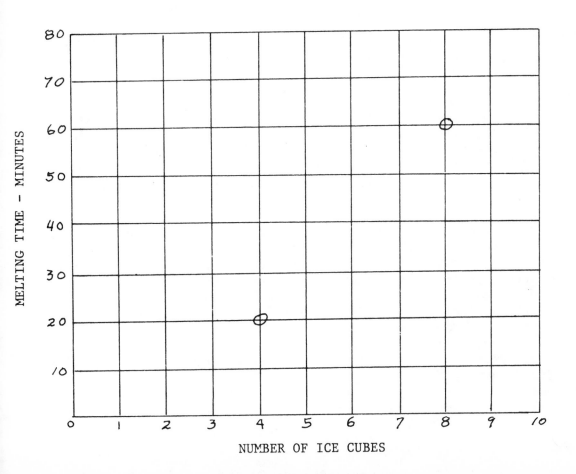

how long you predict it will take three ice cubes to melt. Put one check
in the acceptable column if he marks an X on the vertical line above 3, somewhere below the 20 minute line.

TASK 4 (OBJECTIVE 2): Now say, A test was conducted in which two ice cubes
were added to a jar like those used before. The jar was half full of water.
The melting time was found to be ten minutes. Add these results to the table
of data, and put another dot on the graph to show this added information.
Ask, Would you like to change your prediction for the melting time of three
cubes? Put one check in the acceptable column if he now changes his prediction
for the melting time of three ice cubes to a position representing a time of
approximately 15 minutes. (If his prediction was already 15 minutes, put a
check in the acceptable column if he says "No," meaning that he does not want
to change the position of the X.)

ELEMENTARY SCIENCE STUDY (ESS)

The second major program with which this worktext will deal is the
Elementary Science Study, published commercially by the Webster Division of
the McGraw-Hill Book Company. It is probably somewhat erroneous to call ESS
a "program" because it is, instead, an assemblage of units produced which
were originally intended to supplement an ongoing science program. Even so,
many school districts have taken ESS units and have structured them into a
basic program for elementary and, sometimes, junior high schools.

ESS is one of the major science curriculum projects. It was developed
at the Education Development Center, Inc. in Massachusetts. Funds for the
project were made available from the National Science Foundation. Initial
goals of the ESS development project focused on providing new materials and
methods for improving existing science programs. The rationale was sound
because, when the project was initiated in 1960, science education rarely
reflected a meld of science process and product (skills as well as knowledge).
ESS was intended to reflect the substantive structure of science per se by
permitting students to investigate a number of unique and innovative topics
in manners appropriate to science and their own intellectual capacities and
interests.

The ESS development phase involved over a hundred professional scientists,
teachers, and science educators working cooperatively to develop the materials.
Materials consisted of teachers' manuals, equipment, supplies, films, posters,
and in a few cases, student data collection sheets. After an idea was
turned into an ESS unit, the total unit was taken into classrooms across
the United States and tried in the real world of the elementary or junior
high school. Each unit received trial testing in at least fifty different
classrooms. Problems with units would be isolated, materials revised, and
tried again the following year. Units were commercially published only after
exhaustive field testing.

A major emphasis of ESS is putting materials into the hands of the students. Initially, there may be a good deal of "messing about" or play manipulation of materials and the teacher should accept and appreciate the need for some children to get this out of their systems (in fact, during the preservice training of teachers, it has been a common experience for the writers of this worktext to see methods students doing that very thing with ESS equipment). Elementary students eventually can turn from the "messing about" stage to a more organized investigation of their universe based on the potentials inherent in the unit. Children are natural investigators and their curiosity seems boundless. It becomes a matter of channeling that curiosity into inquiry strategies that have personal payoff from a science standpoint. ESS is a collection of units designed to do this.

ESS units are basically independent of each other. There is no hierarchy in which they must be used. This is but one way in which ESS provides maximum flexibility for the teacher. Units are available in physical science, biological science, earth science, and general skills areas. A unit may emcompass a few days or continue for several weeks. Further, units are found to be functional for more than one grade level, i.e., a unit could possibly be used in grade two, or three, or four. The very nature of the ESS materials provides this kind of flexibility.

ESS materials are largely open-ended as well as being investigative. What does this mean? It means simply that students normally have an opportunity to make decisions about the direction their investigations will take. In the unit entitled Behavior of Mealworms, for example, students initially observe the mealworm (a beetle larva) in terms of its physical characteristics. Following this, they are stimulated to begin asking questions about the behavior of this organism in ways in which they can find out answers for themselves. A student's curiosity about mealworm behavior will lead to his own inquiry, directed toward getting answers. Different students may investigate a wide variety of behavior phenomena. In this way, they learn some of the fundamentals of scientific inquiry as well as answer questions in which they are personally interested.

The ESS teacher must be a competent one. Further, the teacher teaching ESS must be willing to act as a consultant - to help children ask questions, observe, design experiments, and interpret these experiments. Although the ESS teacher should understand the nature of inquiry and open-ended investigation, he/she must also be prepared to admit that he/she knows not the answer and take the position that the teacher and the child can learn together. This, surprisingly perhaps, builds respect between student and teacher and creates a classroom atmosphere with considerably more flexibility than that of the traditional classroom.

How is student progress evaluated in ESS? The people who developed ESS specify that evaluation should be a process that is implicit in the teaching of the ESS unit. This is interpreted as meaning that evaluation is an ongoing process and that appraisals can be provided from direct observation of the student's use of process, his generation of knowledge, and his scientific attitudes. Surely this is a fundamental aspect of excellent teaching in any well-devised science program.

Examples of ESS Flexibility

ESS Unit	K	1	2	3	4	5	6	7	8	9
				Grade Levels at Which Unit Can Be Used						
Light and Shadow	x	x	x	x						
Match & Measure (Skills Unit)	x	x	x	x						
Butterflies	x	x	x	x	x	x				
Geo Blocks (Skills Unit)	x	x	x	x	x	x	x			
Attribute Games & Problems (Skills Unit)	x	x	x	x	x	x	x	x	x	x
Brine Shrimp		x	x	x	x					
Mystery Powders				x	x					
Rocks & Charts				x	x	x	x			
Colored Solutions				x	x	x	x	x	x	
Bones					x	x	x			
Behavior of Mealworms					x	x	x	x	x	
Stream Tables					x	x	x	x	x	x
Gases and Airs						x	x	x	x	

116

However, the teacher who desires to make a critical evaluation of student progress in ESS must carefully analyze those tasks with which the child is engaged and construct his own evaluation instrument or task. If a group of students are absorbed in the business of manipulating and controlling variables (as well could be the case ina unit such as Kitchen Physics), the teacher should make the most of the student's progress in the skills of manipulating and controlling variables. Certainly, if the objective is process, the evaluation should be in the process dimension. As the old adage goes, . . . when teaching bananas we must test bananas . . . not oranges . . . or apples . . . or pomegranates! Evaluation must bear a one to one correspondence with what is taught. In ESS, it would be relatively easy to evaluate student learning in a manner not quite consistent with the teaching because many of the processes used can be masked by the knowledge being created.

Of course, all evaluation should not be accomplished simply to evaluate the student. The teacher can also evaluate her teaching style and the effect of the units by observing students engaged in the business of doing science. One important attribute, often overlooked, is the enthusiasm of the students. If it exists, the teacher has accomplished an important objective - "turning children on" to learning!

Experiencing the
ESS Strategy -

At this time, each methods student will be given a set of experiences designed to familiarize him/her with Elementary Science Study (ESS). Said experiences will include a general inspection of several ESS units.

Further, all students will participate in two or more units from ESS in order that they may experience the program from the child's perspective. Specific instructions will be given in the laboratory for each investigation. Students will be referred to worksheet designed for use with these experiences and incorporated into this section.

An Additional
ESS Assignment -

Subsequent to these activities, each student will prepare a paper, not to exceed 500 words, which adheres to the

following parameters:

1. Each methods student will choose a particular grade level for a regular elementary school situation OR a particular population of children with special needs (e.g., disadvantaged, educable mentally handicapped) and design a one year science program for that population using ESS units.

2. Each methods student will specify the assumptions made in preparing the design (i.e., grade level, type of student population, student needs).

Assignment cont. on page 119.

117

WHAT ARE THE MYSTERY POWDERS?

POWDER NUMBER	WHAT I THINK IT IS	WHY I THINK SO
1		
2		
3		
4		
5		
6		

Methods Worksheet for Mystery Powders (ESS)

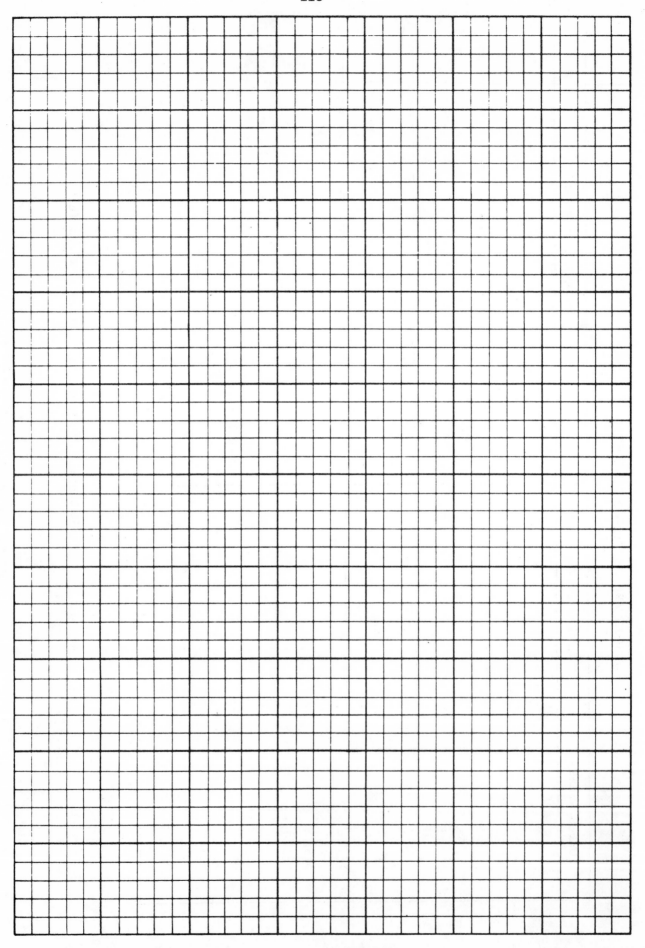

3. The design must incorporate at least five and no more than seven ESS units. Units must be identified by title, content area (e.g., earth science, general skills), and a succinct summary of the activities.

4. The methods student will communicate the rationale for said design from an educational perspective, i.e., why were these units selected for use with children from a general education standpoint. How will they accomplish the goals of the teacher?

SCIENCE CURRICULUM IMPROVEMENT STUDY (SCIS)

The third major program with which this worktext will deal is the Science Curriculum Improvement Study (SCIS), commercially published by Rand McNally & Company of Chicago. SCIS was developed at the University of California, Berkeley with the help of monies contributed by the National Science Foundation.

The SCIS program effectively combines both the process and product sides of science. In fact, the producers of SCIS proclaim that this product blends the knowledge, skills, and attitudes of science into a functional science program. SCIS differs markedly from the programs described thus far in that its activities focus on a conceptual hierarchy.

The developers of SCIS feel that the conceptual portion of science is crucial and that it can be developed as a function of well organized activities. Thus, they feel that a science program should be judged on both its experiential base (process component) and the conceptual hierarchy developed as a function of those experiences.

Each year of the SCIS program finds children experiencing two units of instruction, one in physical science and one in biological science. These can be taught in either order. The major concepts involved throughout are matter and energy in physical science and organism and ecosystem in biology. Woven into all these knowledge components is the important idea of interaction, i.e., the relation among objects or organisms that do something to each other and thereby bring about a change. Thus, interaction relationships are stressed as the student's conceptual knowledge increases in sophistication.

The SCIS program has recently added a single unit called Beginnings, which is taught at the kindergarten level. The purpose of this entire year unit is to develop children's powers of observation, discrimination and description. A wide variety of experiences and activities in the life and physical sciences is used. Through suggested games, puzzles, and other activities, the children develop their abilities to describe and compare objects by their color, shape, size, texture, odor and sound. The concepts of number and volume are introduced. The experiences in this unit contribute to a growing understanding of science and to language development.

Philosophically, the developers of SCIS state the overall objective of the program to be scientific literacy. Said literacy is achieved as a function of the meld of process experience, attitude formation, and conceptual growth of the child. It should probably be added that the conceptual framework of the program agrees with the perceptions of many educators as to the knowledge that is of considerable importance to all literate human beings. Given the rationality of the decisions concerning content and the success of SCIS in developing this knowledge, the elementary school has a powerful and important science program in this one.

SCIS is inquiry oriented, therefore, highly inductive in its learning experiences. For example, in the first grade, children build aquaria with water, sand, plants, fish, and snails. The students observe the aquaria from a number of different perspectives. In a few weeks they notice that a black material has accumulated on the sand in the aquaria. The students' curiosity leads them to wonder what this black "stuff" is and where it came from. Traditionally, the teacher would tell the children that this black material is called detritus and that it originated with the death of animals and plant parts and the wastes of living organisms. Here it would probably end. In SCIS, however, the children pose hypotheses to account for the detritus and compare the growth of seeds in sand in which detritus has been added with growth in sand lacking detritus. Not only do children get a good concept of detritus, but more importantly they begin to perceive the interactions that take place between organisms and between organisms and their abiotic environment. They also receive experiences with intellectual processes such as observation, hypothesizing and experimentation.

Interestingly, SCIS does not rely solely on the laboratory experience for learning and sustaining learning. At various times in the program, field trips are utilized to help facilitate conceptualization. Numerous out-of-class activities lend themselves well to the conceptualization of such ideas as habitat, population, community, plant eater, environment, producer, ecosystem, and pollution. Similarly, discussions are promoted between children and between teacher and children. The discussion might be initiated by the teacher utilizing divergent questions to stimulate a variety of student responses. Or, if the teacher desires to check on the acquisition of knowledge, convergent questions may be used. Children can go to books to gain more information on a number of topics. However, success in SCIS is not predicated on a child's ability to read because the child can always turn to the real three-dimensional world in which he lives for information. Once again, we find a science program suitable for a wide range of student ability levels. In fact, it was observed during extensive use in urban, rural and suburban schools that the earlier editions of the units proved to be particularly helpful as part of the overall effort to improve children's oral language skills. The same potential exists with the current edition. The experience with real and interesting materials is especially effective in the case of disadvantaged or deprived children whose desire to speak and participate in class discussions increases dramatically.

The SCIS teaching format is not organized into tightly structured lessons. Rather, a unit is composed of several parts, each having specific behavioral

OVERVIEW OF THE SCIS PROGRAM*

LEVEL	OVERVIEW	LIFE SCIENCE - CONCEPTS	PHYSICAL SCIENCE - CONCEPTS
1	During the first grade, objectives deal with childrens' observational skills - observation, discrimination, and accurate description (communication). These processes are developed as children care for aquatic plants and animals, raise seedlings, and investigate the properties of nonliving objects.	ORGANISMS organisms habitat birth food web death detritus	MATERIAL OBJECTS object serial ordering property change material evidence
2	The theme of both units is change, observed as evidence of interaction or by the development of an animal or plant. These two units require children to add the mental process of interpreting evidence to the observational skills they developed during first grade. Children work with magnets, batteries, wires, chemicals, photographic paper, pulleys, electric motors, seeds, mealworms, frog eggs, and fruit flies.	LIFE CYCLES growth generation development biotic potential life cycle plant and animal genetic identity metamorphosis	INTERACTION AND SYSTEMS interaction evidence of interaction system interaction-at-a-distance
3	Children observe and experiment with increasingly complex phenomena as they move toward understanding the energy, matter, and ecosystem concepts. In the physical science unit children experiment with solids, liquids, and gases and make and analyze measurements. In the life science unit the children observe the interactions of various organisms within a community of plants and animals considering interdependence.	POPULATIONS population plant eater predator animal eater prey food chain community food web	SUBSYSTEMS AND VARIABLES subsystem solution histogram variable evaporation

#	Description	Life Science Categories	Physical Science Categories
4	In the life science unit, children consider for the first time some of the physical conditions that shape an organism's environment. These investigations make use of the measurement skills and scientific background developed in the physical and life science units during the first three years. The physical science unit introduces techniques for dealing with spatial relationships of stationary and moving objects.	ENVIRONMENTS environment environmental factor range optimum range	RELATIVE POSITION & MOTION reference object reference frame relative position & motion polar coordinates rectangular coordinates
5	Conceptual development continues as examples of energy transfer are introduced in the physical science unit and of food transfer in the life science unit. Children apply the systems concept, the identification of variables, and the interpretation of data with which they have become familiar during the earlier years of the SCIS program.	COMMUNITIES producer photosynthesis consumer community decomposer	ENERGY SOURCES energy transfer energy chain energy source energy receiver
6	The life science unit integrates all the preceding units in both physical and life sciences as children investigate the exchange of matter and energy between organisms and their environment. The physical science unit introduces the concept of the scientific model and thereby opens a new level of data interpretation and hypothesis making. At the same time, the children relate matter and energy to electrical phenomena.	ECOSYSTEMS ecosystem water cycle oxygen-carbon dioxide cycle pollution	MODELS: ELECTRICAL AND MAGNETIC INTERACTIONS scientific model electricity magnetic field

* - Adapted from Science Curriculum Improvement Study (a commercial brochure). School Department, Rand McNally and Company, 1970.

objectives. The parts, in turn, are divided into chapters. Each chapter may contain several activities as well as suggestions for optional, extension lessons.

The SCIS program provides for three stages in a child's learning cycle. These stages, termed exploration, invention and discovery, are based on current Piagetian theory of how children learn. During the exploration stage, students do just that, i.e., they explore the materials with minimal guidance in the form of instructions or specific questions. Since spontaneous learning is limited by the child's perceptions, he needs concept to interpret his observations. Since few children can phrase new concepts by themselves, the teacher at times must provide a definition and a term for a new concept. This constitutes the invention stage of the learning cycle. The third stage, discovery, culminates the cycle in that the teacher gives the students activities in which they discern a new application for a concept. The children's discovery activities reinforce the original concept and enlarge and refine its meaning. In this way, mastery and retention of concepts are aided by practice and repeated, wide application.

One SCIS activity may extend beyond a single class period or several activities may be included in one session. Certain activities, such as the investigation of pulley systems and the magnetic box puzzles are intended for small group or independent study. Other activities are more successful when a larger group or the whole class works together.

Flexibility of the teacher in imperative. So is inservice education of teachers. Successful implementation of SCIS into a total school district is predicated on a successful orientation of teachers to the goals and methodologies of SCIS.

In response to the requests of classroom teachers using the SCIS materials, the developers of the program have produced packets of evaluation materials for each of the twelve units. Each packet contains spirit duplicating masters and specific instructions for evaluating the following aspects of student progress: (1) attitudes in science, i.e., curiosity, inventiveness, critical thinking and persistence); (2) student perception of the classroom environment; and (3) concept/process objectives. Evaluation packets are supplementary to the program and are available from the Science Curriculum Improvement Study, Lawrence Hall of Science, University of California, Berkeley, California 94720.

Use of the evaluation packets is not mandatory for evaluation of student progress. The teacher has the option to use the program's behavioral objectives as a guideline for constructing evaluation measures. Direct observation of student behavior is another available technique. The authors of this worktext would remind any teacher who uses his/her own evaluative measures with SCIS or any other program to be sure that evaluation bears a one to one correspondence with what is taught!

The SCIS program is purchased unit by unit, i.e., two units are purchased separately per year. Unit materials contain supplies and equipment, teacher's guide, and student booklets. Replacement packages are available so that the teacher can replace expended materials and student booklets each year. Living plants and animals are also provided by the publisher where needed.

Experiencing
the SCIS
Strategy –

At this time, each methods student will be given a set of experiences designed to familiarize him/her with SCIS. These experiences will include an inspection of several units, teachers' materials, and evaluation strategies. Further, all students will get direct laboratory experiences with SCIS in order that they may experience the program from the child's perspective. Specific instructions for each investigation will be given in the methods laboratory.

PART VIII

Science Textbook Program Analysis

Performance Objectives

Subsequent to your interaction with Part VIII you will be expected to be able to . . .

1. . . . produce and defend at least six important considerations that should be made when a science textbook is being chosen for use with children in the elementary school.

2. . . . explain how a science textbook can serve a legitimate function in science education by providing conceptual information about science content areas in which children cannot get first hand experiences. Similarly, you will be expected to be able to cite several good examples.

3. . . . identify, write, and/or analyze three kinds of questions often encountered in student texts. These are:

   a. questions measuring the acquisition of factual information.

   b. questions measuring the acquisition of conceptual information.

   c. questions measuring the student's ability to apply newly acquired information.

4. . . . explain why a school district should have its science education objectives sharply in focus before attempting to choose a science textbook program. (In other words, this infers that texts vary - and, they do! Know how they vary and how this could relate to the philosophical setting of the school district. For example, consider such topics as reproduction and evolution and how these topics are presented.)

5. . . . compare the general attributes of a textbook oriented science program to other strategies for science education presented in this course.

6. . . . identify at least two ways that "second generation textbook programs" differ from more traditional science textbook programs.

Possible publishers from which to choose:

Addison-Wesley	D. C. Heath	Harper-Row
American Book Company	Follett	Holt, Rinehart, and Winston
Benefic Press	Ginn and Company	
		Houghton-Mifflin
Bobbs-Merrill	Harcourt Brace Jovanovich, Inc.	Laidlaw

MacMillan   Scott Foresman

Merrill   Silver Burdett

Rand-McNally

Science Textbook Program Analysis

The incorporation of training in (and experience with) textbook analysis
is a practical enterprise for science methods students. Many elementary
teachers, at one time or another, must bear the responsibility for textbook
selection. Similarly, you may have a science textbook program to work from
on your first teaching assignment. It is hoped that this analysis will
familiarize you with the textbook as a teaching device. This methods strategy
should not be inferred as reflecting a total acceptance of the textbook as
a teaching device in the teaching of science. Such is not the case although
textbooks can possess attributes having merit. For example, the textbook can
deal with topics of importance which cannot be presented in an experiential
manner, e.g. volcanism, atomic structure, space exploration and deep sea
oceanography.

Any list of criteria for textbook selection reflects the biases of the
writer(s). Some criteria held dear to the writers might not fit the philosophical mode of the evaluator. Regardless, it behooves anyone considering
textbook programs to compare products judiciously. To ignore the main
objectives of science education in the local school's program is educationally
absurd. Textbooks DO differ and accomplish different ends even when used with
the greatest skill. This is particularly evident when one compares the very
traditional textbook programs with second generation textbook programs.

This assignment requires you to carefully analyze a particular science
textbook program from several important standpoints. This analysis does not
deal with many of the traditional criteria employed in textbook evaluation,
e.g., reading levels. Instead, the criteria reflect, in so far as possible,
the science enterprise itself, the advantages that can be gained by using a
text, some of the disadvantages, and the ways in which the textbook can be
modified in order to provide a sound science education experience in terms of
general education value for children in the elementary classroom.

The specific Textbook Appraisal is found in Appendix B. It should be
carefully prepared and delivered to your instructor in accordance with his
instructions. It will be eventually returned to you.

PART IX

Pros, Cons & A Lesson On Behavioral Objectives

Performance Objectives

Subsequent to your interaction with Part IX you will be expected to be able to . . .

1. . . . produce and write a rationale for the use of behavioral objectives in science education.

2. . . . state or identify at least two criticisms leveled against the use of behavioral objectives in education.

3. . . . state or identify the three fundamental technical elements of an objective that is stated in classic behavioral terms.

4. . . . describe why an objective must be consistent with the knowledge, skill, or attitude desired. Also describe how an author of objectives can guard against such inconsistencies.

5. . . . state why behavioral objectives offer the teacher an opportunity to evaluate his/her own teaching.

6. . . . identify or write at least fifteen (15) performance terms when asked to do so.

7. . . . evaluate behavioral objectives in terms of the classic technical criteria used for writing objectives by stating where errors exist (if they do), rewrite incorrect objectives in order to make them accurate.

8. . . . write one or more objectives in behavioral terms for, (1) factual knowledge, (2) conceptual knowledge, (3) cognitive intellectual processes (cognitive skills), and (4) attitudes.

9. . . . when given a specific problem situation and an assignment to write objectives for that situation, correctly do so.

10. . . . defend the notion that students should be made aware of instructional behavioral objectives at the beginning of any unit or lesson.

Pros, Cons & A Lesson On Behavioral Objectives

Some Pros,
Parameters,
& a Complex
Analysis –

At this moment in time, trememdous amounts of human energy are being devoted to "behavioral objectives" in education. The use of behavioral objectives, in some quarters, is seen as a panacea to the educative process. Using behavioral objectives does, indeed, demand that a teacher know exactly what it is she is teaching and how this teaching is to be evaluated. Where behavioral objectives are used, the teaching can become carefully planned and analytical in nature. No longer is the instructor satisfied with platitudes for objectives in a particular lesson or course of study. Instead, the objectives in a particular lesson are spelled out in terms of terminal performance which is measurable and identifiable.

Let us assume for a moment that we are teaching a unit in science at the sixth-grade level dealing with geologic processes. One of the earth science principles or major ideas assumed to be important might be as follows:

Rocks on the surface of the earth's crust are
attacked and decomposed by the agents of weathering.

The question is: How do we evaluate whether the student intellectually has this principle at his disposal? Below, write an objective that will allow you to measure the student's ability to deal with this principle intellectually, i.e., what can the student do to demonstrate that he does, indeed, thoroughly understand this principle?

Many of those who promote the notion of using behavioral objectives would say that your objective should reflect three main elements. These elements would be: (1) a description of the testing strategy; (2) the specific mode of performance deemed important; and (3) the level of performance necessary before the behavior is deemed acceptable. The authors are willing to express the idea that these three statements can usually be reduced to far simpler terms, namely the elements of (1) the what of the objective; (2) the how of the objective; and (3) the how much of the objective. In other words, what is the student supposed to do, how is he to do it, and how much is he supposed to do?

Let us pose a behaviorally stated objective for the principle you originally wrote one for:

Upon completing the unit of work dealing with geologic processes, the student should be able to define weathering in one written sentence and be able to list three agents of weathering.

Does this behavioral objective fit the criteria specified above? Yes, it does! It tells <u>what</u> the student is to do. It tells <u>how</u> he is to do it. It tells <u>how much</u> he is expected to do. Evidently this makes the objective appropriate. Do you agree or disagree: Why?

The writing of behavioral objectives is no easy task. It is relatively easy to write a particular objective (such as the one above) that contains the three technical elements of behavioral objectives. However, one of the most difficult tasks in the preparation of behavioral objectives is <u>to make certain that the objective is consistent with the knowledge or skill or attitude desired</u>. The objective stated above, although close to the knowledge desired, is in reality a very poor objective if we consider all of the concepts reflected in the principle. It does have the necessary prerequisite technical elements, but it is not necessarily measuring the information needed. It will not stand alone as evidence that the student understands the principle as stated. Merely requiring a definition at this point in time and asking for a list of weathering agents is no guarantee that the student will, in effect, know that the rocks on the surface of the earth's crust are attacked and decomposed by the agents of weathering. We just cannot make that assumption.

It might appear quite superfluous to enter into an argument over the "goodness" of an objective at this point. However, it cannot be considered superfluous in any dimension because, if behavioral objective are good and if they are recommended for use in measuring teaching effectiveness, then they surely <u>must</u> measure what they are supposed to measure. Regardless of how trite this may seem, it is of paramount importance.

Now, let's look back to the original principle and see if we can improve the behavioral objective originally written by the authors. First, we must assume (or test to find out) that the student really understands the terms "rock", "decomposed", and "earth's crust". If these prerequisites have been met, then perhaps the following objective will prove satisfactory:

Upon completing the unit of work dealing with geologic processes, the student will be able to list three important agents of weathering. The student will then specify, in writing, how each agent attacks rocks at the surface of the earth. Similarly, he will be able to write a brief paragraph of no more than 30 words explaining why weathering takes place only where rocks are exposed at or near the surface of the earth's crust.

Does this objective make more sense? Can you identify the critical
technical elements of a behavioral objective in this one? Would these
separate tasks actually provide some measure of a youngster's ability to
function with the originally stated principle? This behavioral objective
may be open to criticism, but it is far superior to the original one given
as an example. Certainly it represents an analysis of the original principle
and what kinds of terminal performance would reflect a competency with it.

You should at this point have a good idea yourself about the constituents of behaviorally stated objectives. You will have another opportunity
to write objectives later on, but first let's examine some comments about
behavioral objectives in general.

We have already noted that the use of behavioral objectives tends to
sharply define those behaviors we desire to work towards in the instructional
process. There is a great deal of good in this concept because it tends to
force teachers to be analytical about what they are teaching. Few other
techniques do this as effectively! It does provide an opportunity to
measure the effects of instruction. Similarly, using behavioral objectives
tends to provide a cohesive force in the classroom which can result in
careful planning and an opportunity for students to finally know what it is
they are supposed to be able to do as a result of their work. This alone
might be enough of an argument for using behavioral objectives because
students have traditionally had to become masters at the guessing game of
trying to figure out what it was they were supposed to be able to do at
the end of a lesson, a unit, or a year's work!

However, let us not end our discussion here with the assumption that
behavioral objectives are all pro and no con! The writers see some inherent
and dangerous problems arising from a totally uninhibited move toward the
use of behavioral objectives.

Some Problems
With Performance
objectives –

You should already have been able to grasp
the fact that behavioral objectives are
not easy to construct. Even those who have
been writing them for some time often find
that some of the ones they have previously written are really not appropriate
to the knowledge or content on which they have been written. In other words,
they may not really measure what the writer was attempting to measure.
Similarly, they may erroneously ask for a behavior with which the student has
no training. For example, he may be asked to form a hypothesis or draw
conclusions when he has had no prior training in either intellectual process.
To be unable to identify errors in such work would eventually prove disastrous
in education. We must not write objectives just for the sake of writing
objectives or because it seems to be the "in thing" to do. If we cannont do
the job well, then we might just be better off not doing it at all.

Thus far we have dealt with the idea of objectives as they relate to
knowledge. How about the other important objectives of working with children
in classrooms? What about skills? Attitudes? It is harsh reality to say
that, unless one is dealing with simple psychomotor skills, the construction
of behavioral objectives for intellectual skill development is much more

difficult than doing it for knowledge. Similarly, constructing behavioral
objectives for attitude development is often thought as an extremely difficult task when one considers many of the complex attitudes that are desirable
as long range goals of education.

Other problems arise from a course of study totally predicated on
behavioral objectives. Dr. J. Myron Atkin[1] warns that the use of behavioral
objectives tends to limit the curriculum developer because if he defines his
goals first, he then has to engineer a program designed to achieve these
goals. This would have a debilitating effect on anyone attempting to develop
an instructional design for certain kinds of cognitive skill development and
attitude formation where sharply defined behavioral objectives are difficult
to come up with. Atkin also points out that most traditional curriculum
developers typically begin with general objectives and then refine the program
through a series of revisions. This creates a situation where an educator
might well produce behavioral objectives in a manner characterized by
"after the fact". Many educators would protest using this technique, but
there are cases where this might actually be a realistic approach. The
authors have spent many months developing units of work which would lead
toward student competency with particular cognitive skills. This was done
intuitively! The sharply defined behaviors expected of students as terminal
performance were not written until after the students were being trained
via this technique. This fact may not reflect well on the writers, but
it does indeed reflect an inherent problem in some kinds of curriculum designs.
Similarly, this problem will not be countered in the near future as long
as there are curriculum developers who tend to operate on gross strategies
(such as developing positive attitudes toward natural resources) which are
not too amenable to operational definition. Surely we cannot expect educators
to stop teaching environmental education because we cannot sharply define
an environmentally-oriented individual operationally.

Regardless of the pros and cons of behavioral objectives, it does appear
pertinent that you have some experiences dealing with behavioral terms as
well as evaluating and writing behavioral objectives so that these skills
might find some transfer to your own classroom.

Performance   Unless one can measure whether a student
Terms –   has met an objective it is meaningless.
                       This speaks poorly of the old standby terms
such as to know, to understand, and to appreciate. We may wish to get a
student to appreciate something but it is virtually impossible to measure an
objective like the following one:

> One of the objectives of this unit is to help
> children learn how to appreciate the native
> wildflowers of Southern Illinois.

Instead, the behaviorally stated objective deals with some observable or
measurable action. It describes what the student should be able to do as a

    1. J. Myron Atkin, "Behavioral Objectives in Curriculum Design: A
Cautionary Note," The Science Teacher, Vol. 35, No. 5 (May 1968), p.29.

consequence of an educational experience. The objective uses performance terms. Some performance terms follow:

construct	select	analyze
compare	describe	evaluate
classify	predict	state
compute	hypothesize	test
write	experiment	design

The following examples indicate how some of these performance terms (and others) can be used behaviorally. Identify, in writing, the performance terms used in the examples below (make sure you also identify those which are inferred as well as overt):

1. Given a multiple choice test item, the student will select the response that correctly defines the term mineral. (What is/are the performance term(s) in No. 1?)

2. The student will be able to write a hypothesis that can be tested experimentally. (Performance term(s)?)

3. The student will write a design of an experiment to test the hypothesis. (Performance term(s)?)

4. Upon completing the unit, the student will be able to correctly classify twenty different line drawings of insects into groups according to insect orders. (Performance term(s)?)

5. The student will show his appreciation for the need to conserve water by inspecting his home and repairing all leaky faucets found there. (Performance term(s)?)

6. While comparing four specimens of reptiles the student will be able to orally state one way in which they are all similar and one way in which each differs from the others. (Performance term(s)?)

Note: Correct responses can be found in Appendix D.

Are They Behaviorally Stated?

Below you will find listed six separate objectives. In the blank in front of the objective write "yes" if the objective is written in behavioral terms and "no" if it is not.

_____1. The student will be able to classify twelve geometric shapes into three separate groups by placing them in three piles, each of which contains closely related kinds.

_____2. The student will orally state an accurate definition of work.

_____3. The student will perceive the relationship between work and energy.

_____4. The student will develop an appreciation of natural resources and form an accurate concept about how he can participate in environmental education.

_____5. The student will prepare a written list that includes three examples of biotic community factors and four examples of abiotic factors.

_____6. The student will demonstrate a positive attitude toward the need for recycling glass by purchasing pop only in reusable containers.

Of the six objectives stated above, four are written behaviorally and two are not. You should have responded "no" to numbers three and four. The term "perceive" is not a performance term nor is "appreciate". There is no way a person can observe directly some else's understanding and appreciation. It is true that these things can be measured, but not directly.

How might you revise numbers three and four so that the desired outcomes can be observed and, therefore, evaluated? Rewrite these below:

Revision:

Revision:

There is no one way to measure either desired outcome. However, regardless of how the evaluation is done, it must be consistent with the knowledge, skill, or attitude desired. If you want to see examples of the revisions, please refer to Appendix D.

Applying What
You Have
Learned -

In the following four problem situations you are asked to write certain instructional objectives in behavioral terms. In each instance yourobjectives are to clearly reflect the appropriate parameters for an objective. Similarly, the objective must correctly reflect the problem. It must be consistent with the operation(s) demanded of the students for whom you are writing the objective. Please be accurate in all dimensions.

PROBLEM I: Your second graders have been involved off and on through autumn with a unit on seasons. They started the first day of fall and ended the first day of winter. They kept a weekly diary of environmental changes as they observed them. One activity was to measure the length of a post's shadow every Monday at exactly 10:30 a. m. (Standard Time).

On completion of the unit you want your students to know (among other things) that their shadows will be longer at a given time in November than they were on September 22. Also, you want them to know that, as fall progresses toward winter, North America is receiving less light energy from the sun and, as a result, it gets colder from September 22 throughout the fall season.

Below write instructional objectives that will measure these important points!

PROBLEM II: Your intermediate class is jsut beginning a unit on energy exchanges in biology. The book they use make a big point of the fact that almost all food energy in the biological world comes directly or indirectly from organisms that contain chlorophyll and carry on photosynthesis. Also, photosynthesis is the process whereby green plants manufacture carbohydrates (sugars and starches) by chemically combining carbon dioxide (CO_2) and water (H_2O) in the presence of chlorophyll and light energy (usually sunlight).

You want your students "to know" three things: (1) what photosynthesis is; (2) the relationship between carbondioxide, water and carbohydrates in the green plant; (3) the relationship between photosynthesis and food energy in the biological world. Write three instructional objectives in behavioral terms that measure the student's knowledge in each of these dimensions. Do this below:

PROBLEM III: You are involved in a unit on soil conservation with your fourth grade students. You have discussed southern Illinois soil conservation problems. You have shown several good films that illustrate soil conservation problems and methods of attacking these problems. Many of these problems and conservation strategies are similar to those observable in the southern Illinois area. Also, you ask the local soil conservationist to come in and talk to the students about these things. He also agrees to lead a field trip to area farms where numerous problems and conservation techniques can be observed.

Write an instructional objective that would allow you to assess whether your students can see the relationship between what they have learned in the classroom with what they see in the field. They must exhibit knowledge about both problems and conservation strategies. Do this below.

PROBLEM IV: You are teaching upper grade students about food chains and food webs in the environment. You illustrate the food chain concept by using an example from the forest community. The example begins with the food producing green plant (an oak) that produces acorns. Some of these acorns are eaten by chipmunks that live on the forest floor. The chipmunk is a first order consumer in this instance. The chipmunk, in turn, is eaten by a coyote who acts as a second order consumer.

Following this simple food chain example you proceed to tell the students that food webs are more complex. The acorn, for example, is not always eaten by the chipmunk. It can be eaten by a squirrel. It could be eaten by a number of different insects. Any of these animals could be preyed upon by others. The same is true for the chipmunk. It could be preyed upon by a fox, a red-tailed hawk, or a great-horned owl. It might also have a couple of worm parasites living in its intestine. These are all factors that should be considered in a food web involving numerous organisms.

You want to find out whether your students understand the <u>difference</u> between a food chain and a food web. Similarly, you also want <u>evidence</u> to indicate that they can reconstruct a simple food chain and a fairly simple food web. Write <u>one</u> instructional objective that will measure <u>both</u> of these desires. Do this below:

Since the beginning of knowledge must be with the
senses, the beginning of teaching should be made with
actual things. The object must be a real, useful
thing, capable of making an impression upon the senses.
To this end it must be brought into communication . . .
if visible, with the eyes; if audible, with the ears;
if tangible, with the touch; if odorous, with the nose;
of sapid, with the taste. First the presentation of
the thing itself and the real intuition of it, then
the real explanation for further elucidation of it.

Johann Amos Comenius - 1657

PART X

The Incidental Science Experience (I.S.E.)*

Performance Objectives

Subsequent to your interactions with Part X you will be expected to be able to . . .

1. . . . define an incidental science experience (I.S.E.) or choose the appropriate definition from a list of alternatives.

2. . . . identify or describe at least two ways the I.S.E. can be used as a vehicle to develop language arts skills.

3. . . . identify at least two reasons why the I.S.E. is a valuable strategy to use with culturally disadvantaged children.

4. . . . cite two examples of situations (other than those described in the reading) that could be defended as I.S.E. and specify how each could be developed into a science learning experience to develop conceptual knowledge.

5. . . . defend the use of a contrived I.S.E. in the classroom and give one example of such a situation stating its application to science education and/or other content areas.

The Incidental Science Experience (I.S.E.)*

The word incidental is defined as being an undesigned feature of something; casual; of secondary importance; accessory. Therefore, an incidental science experience (I.S.E.) might be defined as a casual or undesigned happening related to science instruction in the classroom. Of particular importance is that it need not be of secondary importance. Indeed, for certain purposes the incidental science experience can be extremely important.

What might constitute an I.S.E.? A wide variety of possibilities exist. A child may bring a sack of sea shells to class after a visit to the gulf coast. A meteor might flash across the night sky and receive wide publicity. An animal might have babies during classtime (this has happened more than once). An experiment or demonstration might take a very unplanned turn of events. This could certainly be considered of an incidental (and perhaps unwanted) nature. The teacher might even plan certain "incidental science experiences" for certain students or groups of students.

---

* - The unedited, original version of this section appears here by permission of Instructor; see H. R. Hungerford, "Science Every Day - The Incidental Approach," Instructor, 81, 9 (May 1972), 46.

One very pertinent factor with incidental experiences is that they usually provide high motivation as children seem to be intensely interested in many things that seem discrepant to the normal routine of the classroom. To fail to take advantage of such high interest moments seems unrealistic.

Few science educators would propose that the I.S.E. be allowed to substitute for science curricula that have substance, scope, and sequence. And yet, for certain groups such as culturally deprived children, the incidental experiences, at the primary level particularly, may be of as much value as a more sophisticated science program if used persistently and intelligently. Regardless of the teacher's philosophy, it appears pertinent to explore the values of the I.S.E. so that greater use can be made of it in the classroom.

What will the I.S.E. do for the education process? First, as noted before, they provide an opportunity almost without equal for broadening the experiential backgrounds of children. Many students with very limited experiences with their environment should profit tremendously from this strategy. There should be impact for other content areas as well, e.g., reading.

Second, I.S.E. will provide content of high interest for use in language arts. The use of experience charts in conjunction with incidental science experiences has been used often with outstanding results. Similarly, writing skills can be practiced with little concern for having to motivate children to tackle the assignment. Many experiences find children searching for more information - going to the library to "look things up" or finding someone who has more information to ask for help. Possibilities are quite numerous.

Third, some kinds of incidental experiences find students involved in actual science research that would never have taken place without the opportunity provided by the I.S.E.

An example of said research might help. Some years ago the writer had a student teacher at the middle school level who had occasion to set up what is sometimes referred to as the "Pasteur Spontaneous Generation Experiment". The demonstration is a relatively simple one consisting of five flasks, each containing a nutrient broth in which microorganisms can flourish. In turn, each of these flasks is exposed to the air in a different way using one-hole rubber stoppers and glass tubing. Three of the flasks are set up so that spores in the air can get into the broth and begin growing. Two of the flasks are stoppered so that spores cannot get into the broth. If spores get into the flasks the change in the broth is dramatic within a few days. There can be no question about whether something is going on inside. Both eyes and nose collect information to verify this.

The student teacher set up the demonstration, gave specific instructions to students to carefully observe all flasks, and was horrified to find that growth was taking place in flasks where no one expected mold or bacteria to be found. He came to the writer in near panic to implore him to suggest some way to salvage his demonstration and his pride. It was suggested, since every student was aware of what had happened, that he squarely face the problem with the students and admit something had gone wrong. Also, it was suggested that he explain how the demonstration has been set up so that the students could conceptualize the process. Then, he might ask the students to hypothesize reasons for the failure of the demonstration and to come up with an alternative method of setting it up so it could be tried again, this time with student help. Pride wounded, the student teacher did all of these things. To his great surprise, the students respected his honesty, seriously approached the hypothesizing, and enthusiastically entered into the work involved of setting up a duplicate experiment. The next time there was no failure and when the student teacher left the writer's jurisdiction he unhesitatingly admitted that this had been his most profitable lesson as a student teacher - for him and for the students. Indeed, it was, and it was the direct result of an I.S.E.

One of the concerns of many elementary teachers is their own knowledge about science. There are those teachers that adamantly refuse to cope with an I.S.E. because they feel so inadequate in the affairs of science, particularly unexpected situations like those in question. This is hard to understand because the knowledge is science is so substantial that no one has all the answers. Students who are naturally curious about an object or event are also usually quite willing to research it and report to all concerned (including the teacher). To fail to grasp a classroom situation ripe with positive educational potential seems somehow unethical and, at best, in poor judgment.

How long should a teacher persist with the use of an I.S.E. for purposes of instruction? Certainly, it seems unwise to use it for a period longer than motivation exists. Let the children satisfy their curiosity and then move on. If other than this is done the students may find their curiosity suddenly repressed if they anticipate only hard work and drudgery as a result of expressed interest.

Earlier the point was made that incidental science experiences have value for the language arts. Reference was made to experience charts. Let us take a look at a couple of examples that actually originated in University School at Southern Illinois University. The first is the result of a walk taken by first graders on a warm day in autumn. Many things were observed and upon returning to the classroom some of these were recorded by the students via the experience chart method. The prose elicited from the children follows:

OUR FALL FIELD TRIP

We went on a fall field trip.
We were looking for signs of fall.
The leaves have changed colors.
We saw red, yellow and yellow-green leaves.
Some of the trees were bare.

Patty found some tiny leaves of different colors.
We found some milkweed.
Milkweed seeds fly in the fall.

Another example of the use of experience charts is from the kindergarten. Two very bright boys were intrigued by an ant farm provided by the
teacher. Each day they observed the ants and gave their observations to the
teacher who recorded them on an experience chart. The boys were so interested
in the activity that a copy of the chart was made for each day and the boys
took them home. One experience chart contained the following:

TUESDAY, OCT. 14

Today there is another tunnel along the top.
We found another dead ant today.
The ants are picking up dirt and putting it on top.
We fed the ants.

WEDNESDAY, OCT. 15

The tunnel along the left hand edge is
    longer today.
It looks like a new tunnel is beginning
    in the middle.

If the teacher in a given situation has little response from the children
as far as coming up with incidental science experiences is concerned, she
should not hesitate to suggest that they take advantage of the opportunity
to share finding with fellow students right in the classroom. Failing this
strategy, the teacher should not hesitate to "stack the deck" and provide
high motivational events until the students begin responding with their own.
A gerbil or a pair of gerbils can be extremely motivational in any classroom,
K-8. What child fails to be interested by a box turtle? The thrill of using
a full-size microscope to peer at tiny organisms is apparent at almost any
age. Why not invite a jet pilot to drop by for a classroom visit?

In Summary -   Incidental science experiences are ones
                                that are of immediate concern and have
usually been unplanned. Many incidental experiences can be anticipated in
the elementary school. They are highly motivational. Incidental experiences
can provide a rich source for improving experiential backgrounds in science.
Similarly, they have great potential as vehicles in language arts instruction.
Teachers should not be reticent about using an I.S.E. because she is fearful
of her own inadequacies. The I.S.E. should not exceed the childrens' interest.

PART XI

Science In Special Situations: Environmental Education (E.E.)

Performance Objectives

Subsequent to your interactions with Part XI you will be expected to be able to . . .

1. . . . cite evidence to explain how science education and EE differ. Both content and values should be referred to in this discussion.

2. . . . cite evidence to support the idea that the structure of EE is interdisciplinary in nature.

3. . . . analyze any EE activity and communicate the extent to which it relates to one or more of the following: (A) science, (B) social studies, (C) math, (D) language arts, (E) problem solving, and (F) values clarification.

4. . . . identify and/or describe those attributes for environmental literacy listed in the worktext under each of these headings: (A) cognitive knowledge, (B) cognitive process, and (C) affect.

5. . . . locate (using secondary sources) and describe one or more EE activities and/or programs available for use with elementary school students (Gds. K-8). This description should include appropriate grade level(s), content used, methods used, and appropriateness for developing environmental literacy attributes.

6. . . . choose a specific environmental issue (e.g., energy consumption, air pollution, whale management, abortion, endangered water fowl species) and design activities which could be used with children in a unit on that topic. Further, you will be expected to communicate precisely how that activity relates to the development of environmental literacy.

7. . . . succinctly discuss the very definite relationship that exists between human values and environmental issues.

8. . . . defend the idea that instruction in EE should help a student clarify his/her values to the point where that individual is willing to act on those environmentally-related values.

9. . . . conduct a values clarification session using either assigned or self-selected activities in such a manner as to provide for the actual clarification of personally held values. This infers, in part, that you will be proficient in carefully selected question asking strategies.

10. . . . identify and/or describe the attributes of environmental action as presented in the worktext, i.e., categories, levels, and constraints.

11. . . . analyze environmental action anecdotes and determine the appropriateness of said actions using the action constraint questions found in the worktext.

Science In Special Situations: Environmental Education (E.E.)

Environmental Education is that aspect
of man's education that deals with
culturally-imposed, ecologically-
related problems in man's environment
. . . further, the acquisition and
application of human values as related
to the cultural use and misuse of
biotic and abiotic resources.

H.R.Hungerford
R.A.Litherland — 1975

The Many Faces of
Environmental
Education —

Environmental education is not synonymous
with science education. In fact, there
is a great deal of argument about the
exact boundaries of this "discipline".
Why, then, include environmental education in a science methods book? There
are several reasons. Among these is the fact that research tells us that,
where science is taught on a departmentalized basis, that it is the science
teacher who must assume the responsibility for environmental education over
50% of the time. Further, a number of elementary school science programs
delve into the general area of environmental education. And, finally, a
number of states have passed legislation making it mandatory to teach
environmental education (EE) and, therefore, the writers of your worktext
feel that some background information could prove helpful to you as a
teacher of EE.

The definition for EE found above is one that is used in an EE program
for the middle school grades. It is quite specific in its boundaries but
it gives one an opportunity to perceive that EE is interdisciplinary and
not the sole stepchild of science.

What are the disciplinary facets of EE? First, of course, is the social
studies component (please see the diagram on the following page). Given
that EE subsumes particular social and/or cultural problems, the social studies
implications are clear. The roots of environmental problems are found in
the cultural use or misuse of resources. Further, as with technology,
decisions concerning the use of resources are value laden. In fact, if
there were no differences of opinion concerning the management of biophysical
resources, no environmental issues would exist.

A second component of environmental education is science. EE must have
science as one of its supporting bases. The entire spectrum of resources is

science-related. Knowledge concerning mineral resources, for example,
is largely a function of geology - population demographics a function
of geography - knowledge of the atmosphere a function of the atmospheric
sciences - knowledge of the transfer of food energy and community
structure a function of ecology and so on.

EE is also a function of language arts. The very communication of
problems and value positions is an integral part of EE. Similarly,
numerous research and communication skills are brought to bear on EE
when students are permitted to conduct and report on research into specific
environmental problems. In fact, there are isolated and highly competent
language arts teachers who use - successfully - environmental education

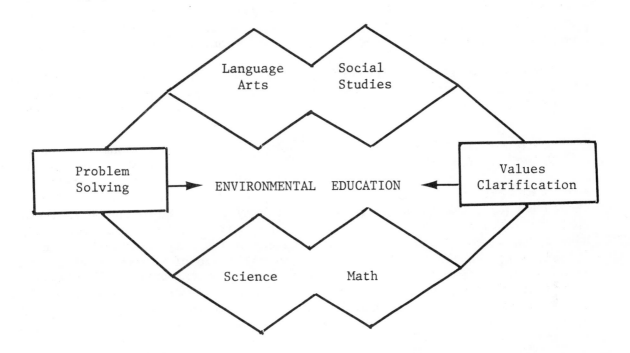

as a vehicle to develop a wide array of language arts skills. Their rationale
is simple in that they believe that students should function with their
language in a context that is as close to the real, three-dimensional world
as possible. EE provides this opportunity.

Mathematics plays an integral role in EE. It is brought to bear in many
science related environmental problem solving activities as well as having
environmental application in the social studies. How can one manipulate
population data, for example, without using math skills? Math must be
applied in surveys, questionnaires, and opinionnaires. It comes into play
in a myriad of ways, e.g., graphing, figuring percentages, and other mathematical treatments of data.

What of other educational components of EE? There are several of
tremendous importance. It was noted above that decision-making regarding
resource use was value laden. Much is currently being made of value clar-

ification in education. What better medium than environmental education
to permit the student to inspect, modify, defend, and act on his own personal values? Similarly, environmental education should have a dramatic
socializing influence on students. The opportunity to relate personally
to other human beings as well as to personally meaningful social problems
should have considerable influence on a person's self-image and his mode of
interacting with other school-community members.

Lastly, EE can allow for the continued development of cognitive skills
(processes). Giving the individual an opportunity to become involved in
autonomous research and environmental problem solving provides an opportunity
for training and practice with numerous processes. Included could be such
skills as observation, comparison, classification, controlling variables
and collecting data (in surveys, opinionnaires, and questionnaires), drawing
conclusions, making inferences, and writing recommendations.

Thus, we perceive the interdisciplinary nature of environmental education.
EE is definitely a special situation for science but science is only one
component in a multifaceted and important aspect of education for children.

Environmental Literacy,
Objectives for EE - *
                                A major objective of environmental education
                                must be to develop an environmentally liter-
                                ate citizenry that is both competent to take
action on critical environmental issues and willing to take that action.
Should one be prone to argue with this objective, it should be pointed out
that, if educators' objectives are anything less than this, they may well
have opted in favor of environmental anarchy and a deterioration of the
biosphere to the point where man may pay the price of massive mortality in
order to reach some sort of equilibrium with the environment. Ecological
data indicate that, should this mortality occur, it must be understood that
any subsequent equilibrium would be achieved at a level far lower in population
carrying capacity than would be the case if man took sincere and ecologically
compatible actions now.

Environmental literacy, then, appears to be both a rational and critical
goal of education. The writers believe that discrete objectives for environmental literacy can be classified under three headings. These are: (1) cognitive knowledge, (2) cognitive process, and (3) affect. These literacy
components are listed below. A careful reading of them is required in order to
conceptualize the entire spectrum of environmental literacy. They follow:

Cognitive Knowledge Component:

Human beings who have acquired the cognitive knowledge component can be
identified as citizens who . . .

1. . . . have knowledge of those ecological concepts which bear upon a

---

* - This section adapted from Chapter II of H. R. Hungerford and R. Ben
Peyton. Teaching Environmental Education. Portland, Maine: J. Weston
Walch, Pub., 1976.

thorough understanding of communities, ecosystems, and man as an ecological factor.

2. . . . are aware of major environmental issues and can communicate the ecological implications of those issues.

3. . . . are aware of how they personally interact with the environment and the implications of these interactions.

4. . . . have knowledge of the impact of man's cultural activities on the environment, e.g., business, industry, agriculture, government, consumer practices, religion.

5. . . . have knowledge of the role played by differing human values in the creation of environmental issues and can communicate the need for value clarification as one step in the solution of environmental problems.

6. . . . have knowledge of and the ability to communicate the need for environmental action strategies, i.e., persuasion, legal action, political action, consumerism, and ecomanagement.

Cognitive Process Component:

Human beings who have acquired the cognitive process component can be identified as citizens who . . .

1. . . . have the ability to apply ecological principles to an analysis of and the solution of environmental issues.

2. . . . have the ability to use both primary and secondary source inquiry strategies to obtain information on environmental issues, i.e., have the ability to use cognitive skills in environmental problem solving.

3. . . . have the ability to use those skills involved in environmental action strategies, e.g., consumerism, political action, etc.

4. . . . have the ability to logically inspect personally-held values in the light of new information.

Affect Component:

Human beings who have acquired the affect component can be identified as citizens who . . .

1. . . . have a desire to maintain an environmental perspective - or ethic - consistent with ecological stability, i.e., a willingness to strive for a homeostatic relationship with the biosphere.

2. . . . are willing to enter into the process of values clarification.

3. . . . are willing to use environmental action strategies in an effort to solve environmental issues.

Values Clarification
Comments and Strategies -   *   Although environmental literacy is a
combination of knowledge, skill, and
attitudes (values), there is not enough
time in this course to deal with all in detail. However, the business of
values clarification in EE is critical enough to demand at least a modicum
of attention.

The values one holds are a function of that person's socio-cultural
background and the knowledge held concerning the issue in question. Research
in EE tends to indicate that new knowledge will, indeed, influence values. It
also indicates that, when a student does in-depth research into an issue,
that research will usually result in either the modification of existing
values or the attainment of a number of new value positions or both. This
statement correctly notes that a human being may well have several value
positions relative to one particular issue.

Only recently has values clarification received educational status in
the United States. Proponents of values clarification believe that the
clarification process has numerous benefits for students. Among these are:
(1) to make the individual more purposeful, (2) to help people sharpen their
critical thinking skills, and (3) to help people have better interpersonal
relations. Values clarification is often recommended for use in areas such
as sex education, career education, drug education, religious education, and
EE.

Environmental literacy is very dependent on the individual's continual
evaluation of personally held values. This evaluation probably goes on
continuously, prompted by new information or new experiences with the environment. Teachers can stimulate a more rapid evolution of personally held
values by providing information and experiences designed to do exactly that.
This, of course, tends to infer that the professionals doing the stimulating
probably hold some preconceived notion about the direction in which those
values should evolve. Although there are many who would argue this inference,
it is probably, in the final analysis, true. We would like very much to be
able to provide settings in which we remain entirely neutral as far as
students' values are concerned. But, we know full well that our biases will
eventually creep into both the process itself and the setting within which
that process is taking place. As noted earlier, we believe that an environmentally literate human being is one who is willing to maintain an environmental ethic consistent with ecological stability (homeostasis). This is a
value! It is a philosophical bias, regardless of how defensible it is! Values
clarification activities produced by the authors tend to try and nudge the
student in that direction. Certainly, we do not apologize for this admission.
We simply wish to make the very important point that the so-called "neutrality"
which the educator is supposed to represent probably does not exist - even
under the best of circumstances.

Values cannot be taught in the traditional sense. When people go through
the process of values clarification they do so in a very private and personal

* - This section adapted from Chapter III of H. R. Hungerford and R. Ben
Peyton. Teaching Environmental Education. Portland, Maine: J. Weston
Walch, Pub., 1976.

ITS JUST A MATTER OF VALUES

manner. No amount of preaching or intimidation will make a person truly accept a value position. Of course, students might verbalize a particular value, or behave as if they had that value in order to avoid ridicule or punishment. But, this mode of behavior is artificial and will be reversed as soon as the threat is removed. The values that count are those that human beings accept and act on freely and consistently. Therefore, it is crucial that the teacher attempt to promote an education climate in which values can be chosen freely from available alternatives, tested against logic, and acted on.

A number of values clarification activities for EE exist. Values can often be inspected and clarified as a function of inquiry strategies in EE. Other strategies also exist. Numerous discussion activities lend themselves well to values clarification. At these times the teacher must be quick to ask the right questions. Questioning is critically important. Depending upon the situation, questions could take the form of the following:

- Why did you answer as you did?
- Should you or the class get involved in this controversy? Why?
- What is the problem? Why does it have environmental implications?
- Why do you prefer one alternative over the other?
- Do you think your choices are the best possible? Why? Why not?
- What are your own priorities concerning technological expansion?
  - Toward nature? Are these priorities compatible? Why? Why not?

Many activities are surprisingly easy to conduct and yet yield some very serious thinking on the part of students. An activity such as the one which follows may prove productive:

A Problem for the Johnsons

In 1958, Mr. & Mrs. W. R. Johnson purchased a home on the outskirts of Bigsville for $19,850. Over the next few years, land and building values increased so that the Johnsons felt perfectly comfortable when they finished the basement and added a garage and workroom for Mr. Johnson.

In 1967, the Bigsville Airport Authority condemned nearly 1000 acres of land just a mile north of the Johnson home. In 1973, an international airport was in service where there had been only farm land before.

Since the development of the airport, highway construction and traffic has increased over 100 times. Noise levels are, at times a serious problem. Crime has increased over 300% and property values have decreased greatly. Today, the Johnson residence is barely worth $20,000 even with the additional money invested and a high rate of inflation.

The biggest problems for the Johnsons are economic and psychological. The Johnsons did not anticipate living near a jetport, nor did they anticipate an increase in crime and noise levels. Certainly, they did not anticipate a tremendous decrease in property values.

Possible Questions:

1. What options are available to the Johnsons?

2. What responsibilities, if any, does the Bigsville Airport Authority have in this situation?

3. Is there a "way out" of the situation for the Johnsons? If so, what are the alternatives?

4. Assume that the entire area was equally disturbed by the airport. Would an environmental action citizens' committee be able to help? How would such a group go about getting something done? What if the committee finds out that their only hope is to conduct themselves in an illegal manner? Should they continue their efforts? Why? Why not?

The value of the above activity is, in part, determined by the teacher's ability to ask those questions that probe the students' values and gives them an opportunity to inspect the bases of those values. Excellent class discussions can result from such an anecdote and the teacher must be cautious in deciding to what extent to permit the discussion to "heat up" if there are sharp differences of opinion (differing values across the class).

Now, what about some of your own environmental values? The following activity has been designed to demonstrate the divergence of values that can exist in both pre and inservice teacher populations. It has been used many times with considerable success. Please complete this brief activity, following directions carefully.

Let's Compare Values

This activity is designed to let you compare a few of your environmental values with those of your peers. Below, you will find a list of eight (8) statements with which you may agree or disagree. Following each is a number line ranging from "strongly disagree" to "strongly agree". You are asked to circle the number of the response which best reflects how you feel about the statement. Please do this before going on to the rest of the activity.

1. The killing of deer by hunters is an important part in keeping deer herds healthy.

X	X	X	X	X
Strongly Disagree	Disagree	Neutral	Agree	Strongly Agree

2. The great whales don't belong to any nation and, therefore, any nation that wants to hunt them should have the right to do so.

X	X	X	X	X

3. No human female should be permitted to have more than two children.

X	X	X	X	X

4. Laws should be passed making car pools mandatory in large towns and cities.

X	X	X	X	X

5. The recycling of steel, aluminum, and glass should be mandatory even if it is not currently profitable.

X	X	X	X	X

6. Air pollution standards should be lowered in order to get better gasoline mileage in automobiles.

X	X	X	X	X

7. Only those people who live alone or have special problems should be allowed to keep a dog or a cat because of the tremendous amount of food energy consumed by pets.

X	X	X	X	X

8. Nuclear power plants should be built at the fastest possible pace to produce needed electrical energy.

X	X	X	X	X

Now, on the next page you will find a summary chart. After everyone in the class has responded to the items above, add up the class responses in each category for each statement. This will clearly show whether there is a wide variation of values within the class for a given statement. If this proves to be the case, a discussion might determine the reasons for this.

Summary

No. Strongly Agree	No. Disagree	No. Neutral	No. Agree	No. Strongly Agree
1.				
2.				
3.				
4.				
5.				
6.				
7.				
8.				

Postsummary Discussion:

1. Analyze those statements for which there is a wide difference of opinion. Why do these differences exist? What are the logic bases for these values positions? Are these values positions ecologically sound? Why? Why not?

2. What seems to be the solution to an environmental issue where there are strong and differing value positions?

3. Could it be possible that differing value positions are the very things that create environmental issues in the first place? Why? Why not?

Can Students Become Involved in Environmental Issues?

Regardless of how one goes about the business of EE, the eventual outcome should be a citizen who is both willing and able to take action in the solution of environmental issues. Unfortunately, there are few programs that actually attempt to develop environmental action skills in students. The reason for this state of affairs is not clear but it is probably due to the fact that most EE programs go about the business of making the student environmentally aware with the assumption that this will lead to action. This assumption is probably incorrect and students should be given direct instruction in environmental action strategies.

Training in environmental action strategies should include information on the wide array of possibilities that exist for positive action. These range from individual citizen action to group action. Further, the power of group action should be stressed in that coalitions of human beings can usually exert more influence than can the individual, working alone. Similarly, group action can vary from that expressed by a student council or a neighborhood coalition to that expressed by international organizations like UNESCO or Ducks Unlimited.

The categories of action and the skills inherent in these categories should be dealt with. These categories, as noted earlier, include persuasion, political action, legal action, consumerism, ecomanagement, or combinations of these. Every elementary school youngster could get involved in all of these with the exception, perhaps, of legal action. Examples of said involvement will be found later in this section.

Of considerable importance are the constraints that must be placed on action. These constraints infer that there are some serious questions that must be attended to before an action is taken. The writers of this worktext, working with other curriculum developers in EE, have identified a number of questions that should be attended to before an action is decided on. They follow:

1. Is there sufficient evidence to warrent action on this issue?
2. Are there alternative actions available for use? What are they?
3. Is the action chosen the most effective one available?
4. Are there legal consequences of this action? If so, what are they?
5. Will there be social consequences of this action? If so, what are they?
6. Will therebe economic consequences of this action? If so, what are they?
7. Are my (our) values consistent with this action?
8. Do I (we) understand the procedures necessary to take this action?
9. Do I (we) have the skills needed to take this action?
10. Do I (we) have the courage to take this action?
11. Do I (we) have the time needed to complete this action?
12. Do I (we) have all of the other resources needed (other than the above) available to make this action effective?
13. What are the ecological implications of this action?

A part of the training students get on environmental action could involve their analyzing the actions of others subsequent to training in categories, levels, and the constraints which should be placed on action. In particular, students should have an opportunity to analyze actions in terms of the key questions listed above. An example of an anecdote which could be analyzed follows:

Drawing Attention to Nuclear Power

   One man's protest against nuclear power plants made headlines
on Washington's Birthday. Instead of chopping down a cherry
tree, Samuel H. Lovejoy - a twenty-seven-year-old college
student and organic farmer - toppled a 500 foot tower being
built in connection with a $1.3 billion Northeast Utilities
nuclear power plant at Montague, Massachusetts. Unlike the
Fox - an anonymous conservation commando who committed acts of
vandalism against polluting industries in the Midwest but was
never caught - Lovejoy made his point by cutting the guy wires
that held up the tower and immediately surrendered to police.
In a four-page typed statement, he took full responsibility
for the sabotage, which he hoped would set people to thinking
about the dangers of nuclear power. He did elicit reactions.
Many young people were for him; most conservative New Englanders
were shocked, and conservation groups deplored this kind of
protest and disassociated themselves from it. *

  *
   - Taken from the May, 1974 issue of Audubon, page 107.

          Interestingly, this anecdote points out that there are some
serious questions which can be raised about certain kinds of actions. Not
all actions are appropriate.

     Whether or not students get involved in environmental action must depend
upon the extent to which they are capable, the administrative perspective of
the school, and the courage and tenacity of the teacher. Children - in
particular those of middle school age - are very able to get involved in
issues which are surrounded by considerable controversy. In these situations
the teacher can expect some criticism, particularly from those segments of
the population which represent values running counter to those of the students.

     Below, you will find a number of actual case-studies of action projects
promoted by students and/or teachers. In each case, the categories of action
which apply are identified.

          Student Action Anecdotes:

Categories	Action
Persuasion Political Action	Middle school students in southern Illinois become involved in plans to dam a particularly scenic and scientifically rich canyon. Students wrote to government officials at the state and national levels. They prepared editorials for the local newspapers. The canyon was not dammed and they felt that they had a part in the decision-making process.

Ecomanagement	Middle and senior high students in a midwestern community became concerned about the eastern blue-bird as an endangered species. Over forty nest boxes were constructed in an effort to improve bluebird population levels in the area. All nest boxes were installed on rural university property. Followup observations indicated that the project was a success.
Persuasion	Middle school students in another midwestern school became distraught over the amount of water being lost due to leaky faucets in their school. They took careful measurements and determined that the annual loss costed taxpayers in excess of $100. The students put up a poster communicating their findings (without the knowledge of the teacher) and the faucets were repaired within twenty-four hours.
Ecomanagement Persuasion	Students in an eastern urban area became concerned about the depressing environment around their junior high school. They gained permission to landscape the grounds, plant gardens in bare areas, and beautify the area generally. A school-wide campaign was conducted to get students to help protect seed beds and saplings. Community support grows for the project.
Ecomanagement Persuasion	Art students in a Missouri elementary school decided that the exterior of their school was being defaced at an alarming rate. With the cooperation of their art teacher, they got permission to paint murals on the metal panels being defaced and worked to get other students interested in the aesthetic potential of the school site.

An Analysis of Sample EE Strategies – Below you will find two sample strategies which have been widely used in EE. These activities are incorporated here for two reasons. First, you may want to adapt them for use in your own classroom. Second, you are asked to critically analyze these strategies to determine the extent to which they reflect the interdisciplinary nature of EE. In other words, to what extent do each of these incorporate problem solving skills, values clarification, math, science, language arts, and/or social studies?

Resource Worksheets

A natural place to begin dealing with environmental problems is in the students' own geographic area. Many teachers prefer to have students generate data and inductively derive generalizations concerning specific, local

environmental problems or management practices. One technique which successfully involves the student in such investigation is called the "resource
worksheet". Students are given data collection worksheets covering one of
a number of different environmental topics, e.g., the business district of
the community, the city water works, the sewage plant, the garbage dump,
or local strip mining practices. Students collect data individually or in
small groups and bring this information back to the class as a whole.
Numerous extension activities can grow out of this strategy including action
projects aimed at improving resource management at the local level. One
such worksheet entitled "The City Water Works" follows:

City Water Works Worksheet

1. Briefly describe the geographic location of the city water works.

2. What is the source of raw water for the city and where is this
   source located?

3. Are there alternative sources of water? What are they and where
   are they located?

4. Make a simple diagram of the flow of water from its source to the
   final storage tanks. Include each step in the treatment process.

5. Are there any special treatments needed before the raw water is
   fit for human consumption? If so, what are they?

6. Are the facilities large enough to maintain an adequate supply of
   water 24 hours a day? What is the evidence for this?

7. In the case of fire or other emergency, is there an adequate reserve
   of water?

8. Does the water treatment plant have sufficient capacity to meet
   growing demands for water . . .

   next year? _____   next five years? _____

   next two years? _____   next ten years? _____

9. Can the source of water supply enough raw water for the growing
   demands over these same time spans?

10. What training is provided for city water works operators?

11. Home owners are charged for the water they use. Is the city using
    the most economical method(s) for providing water to home owners?
    What other methods might be available?

12. What problems, if any, do the water works employees identify as
    being related to local water consumption, supplies, pollution, etc.?

13. Do you have any suggestions as to how you or your class might help solve any existing water resource problems? Might it be possible to sponsor a community water use awareness campaign in order to get home owners to reduce water consumption?

Determining Water Consumption

The analysis of a person's own water consumption is an excellent followup activity to the one described above. This strategy could also be used without the prerequisite of investigating the local water works. In any event, this particular investigation has been used successfully in the intermediate grades. It is a proven values clarification exercise and can result in better water management practices in the home.

Determining Water Consumption

How much water do you use? How much water does your family use? How does this compare with other homes in the community? Is this water consumption necessary? How much water could be conserved throughout your community if every home owner and renter chose to use the minimum amount needed for good health and cleanliness? How much could be conserved nationally? These are a few of the questions you can attempt to answer through this activity.

The first task is to determine the weekly consumption of water in your own home. Below you will see a list of uses of water. By carefully observing and measuring water consumption in your own home, complete this computation. (You may need to figure out some interesting ways to make some of these measurements!) Be sure to include all uses you can think of besides those listed here.

Home Water Consumption

Use	Gallons Needed Per Week
Drinking and food preparation	
Dish washing	
Clothes washing	
Car washing	
Bathing, showering, general washing	
Toilet flushing	
Garbage disposal (if mechanical)	
Watering grass, gardens, etc.	
Water for pets - drinking, bathing, etc.	
Water lost from leaking faucets	
Other _____	
Total gallons used per week:	

Divide the "Total gallons used per week"
by the total number of persons in your
home. This will give you the average
number of gallons used per person per
week.

Number of gallons per person per week . . . _____

The second task is to determine the <u>minimum</u> amount of water
needed for all uses in your home. It is sometimes amazing to
discover that considerable water can be saved by changing a few
personal habits, repairing leaking faucets, etc. How much is
really needed? Compute the minimum needs below:

Minimum Home Water Needs

Use   Gallons Needed
___   Per Week

Drinking and food preparation   _____
Dish washing   _____
Clothes washing   _____
Car washing   _____
Bathing, showering, general washing   _____
Toilet flushing   _____
Garbage disposal (if mechanical)   _____
Watering grass, gardens, etc.   _____
Water for pets - drinking, bathing, etc.   _____
Water lost from leaking faucets   _____
Other _____   _____

Minimum gallons needed per week: _____

Again, divide this sum by the total
number of people in your home to get
an average.

Minimum number of gallons per person per week _____

At this time subtract the minimum number
of gallons per week from the original number
of gallons per person per week. This will
will give you the amount of water that can
be conserved per person per week.

How many gallons can you save
per person per week?   _____ gallons

How does this figure compare with the water savings computed by
other students in your class?

What seems to be a reasonable number of gallons that could be
conserved by all people you know? This will be determined by
discussing average water uses in homes in your immediate area
(e.g., other members of your class).

How much water could probably
be saved per person per week
in your community?   _____ gallons

At this point you are to find out the population of your community. Multiply the newest average number of gallons saved by the
population of your community. This will give you an estimate of the
amount of water that could be conserved in your community alone.

Estimate of amount of water
that could be conserved each
week in the community: _____ gallons

Next, compute the number of gallons that could be conserved in
the community each year. Simply multiply your last figure by 52.

Estimate of amount of water
that could be conserved each
year in the community: _____ gallons

Would this estimate of the water that could potentially be saved
have an impact on water resources in your area or community? Would
it conserve the underground water supply? Might it help solve a
critical water shortage? Would it mean less stress being placed on
the municipal water works? On the sewage disposal system? You
might call the water company and the sewage disposal facility and
inquire about these last two factors.

How would your estimate of water consumption savings in the home
look on a national basis? It is a relatively simple matter to compute
this. There are approximately 200,000,000 people in the U.S. today.
However, remember, if there is an error in your original estimate, you
will be multiplying that error by 200,000,000!

The earth as a life-support system is deteriorating.
This the reader must understand clearly, in case he
hasn't noticed or has been persuaded otherwise. In
some respects our children's world will be better than
ours, but on balance it will be uglier, less interesting,
and more dangerous. This is not a pleasant fact to face,
but denial is not a sufficient response to the problem.

R. Thomas Tanner - 1974

PART XII

Science In Special Situations: Children With Special Needs

Performance Objectives

Subsequent to your interactions with Part XII, you will be expected to be able to . . .

1. . . . explain why the classic criteria of I.Q. and reading ability are ineffective for identifying many gifted children. You will be expected to specifically note "gifted attributes" not generally isolated by traditional I.Q. and reading test instruments.

2. . . . briefly explain how science instruction can provide success for a wide range of student ability levels in the elementary school.

3. . . . specifically cite several attributes of a teacher who can provide success for a wide spectrum of students including both slow and gifted using science as a vehicle.

4. . . . take any one major concept that has general education value for children (e.g., sexual reproduction, interaction, energy transfer, the ecosystem) and demonstrate an ability to communicate how that concept can be inductively generated at various ability levels.

5. . . . explain why the disadvantaged child's educational values may prove to be the most educationally debilitating attribute reflected by that student.

6. . . . analyze and react orally or in writing to the following true episode: "A few years ago, the senior author of your worktext was principal of a 1000 student junior high school in the midwest. One of the students was a black girl who manifested a set of values inconsistent with the values of the school and its educational program. Many problems for the girl - and the school - resulted. The writer, along with the girl's counselor, decided to visit the home and attempt to communicate with the girl's mother (the father was not in the home) the school's need for parental cooperation. After arriving at the girl's home, the two educators were met by the girl's mother and her older sister, a reputed prostitute. A friendly but forceful effort was made to help the mother and the girl's sister perceive the need for value modification on the part of the junior high student. The mother was noncommital and the girl's sister laughed out loud. No value modification resulted!"

In your analysis, logically hypothesize as to why the school's principal failed in his mission. Also, attempt to suggest a strategy that might have been more successful in modifying the girl's values.

7. . . . list and defend the choice of at least four (4) different
strategies that could be used to broaden a child's experiential background
in science.

8. . . . explain why the technique of using the disadvantaged child's
own environment to facilitate educational achievement could be detrimental
to the child if carried too far.

9. . . . choose any one category of children with special needs, identify
the specific needs of those children, and design a science teaching strategy
(in the form of a teaching unit) which helps meet those needs. You must
be able to defend the educational assumptions which are reflected in the unit.

Science In Special Situations: Children With Special Needs

Through proper adaption of the elementary science
curriculum to the needs of this large portion of our
children, we may bring about an enrichment of their
lives which, in turn, will benefit our entire community. We have, so far, failed to tap America's
greatest resources, the creative skills and abilities
of all its children. Among these disadvantaged children, there is a large reservoir of future high-level,
professional, and skilled personnel, if we learn how
to help them realize this potential.

Samuel Malkin - 1964

It seems a shame to have to categorize children as "slow" or "disadvantaged", or "gifted", or this . . . or that! Such labels have a tendency,
oftentimes, to operate in a detrimental fashion for both teachers and
students. Far too often teachers are prejudiced against "special populations" of children and, far too often, children perceive how they have
been categorized and function accordingly, irrespective of how they could
function from a socio-educational standpoint.

The writers must assume, simply from a time and energy standpoint, that
these detrimental conditions do not operate in classrooms - knowing full
well that this is not the case. For pragmatic reasons we will assume that
there are no bigoted teachers and that education's labels do not manifest
themselves in detrimental and self-debilitating behavior.

This section supposedly deals with the topic of "science for children
with special needs". In so doing, the writers are compelled to deal with
other educational components as well since science education as such does
not and cannot operate in a sociocultural vacuum. Science offers tremendous
opportunities for many children with special attributes but, by itself, it
can provide no miracles and no panaceas!

Science for "Slow"
and "Gifted"
Children –

If the reader is aghast at seeing both "slow" and "gifted" subsumed under the same heading it would not be too surprising. This would be the case, particularly if the classic criteria were used in identifying these children, i.e., they are sorted out and labeled according to reading ability and I.Q. Even though these two criteria are useful in certain diagnostic situations, they often end up being the sole conditions under which labels are applied. If this be the case, what happens to the child who cannot read for psychological reasons and, therefore, functions poorly on the mental ability instrument? What happens to the child who has "better than average" cognitive potential (in any one of a number of areas) but, because of a weak cultural background, cannot cope successfully with those I.Q. test items that demand a cultural literacy? Is this child <u>expected</u> to perform at a high cognitive level? <u>Will</u> the child perform at a high cognitive level? Remember, there is research evidence to support the notion that children tend to perform in ways we <u>expect</u> them to perform. Needless to say, this generalization is not an educational absolute; it is simply a general predictor of performance. Even so, it bears tremendous implications for the classroom teacher.

Fortunately, educators are beginning to sense that reading per se and I.Q. performance per se are only two attributes of the human organism. We perceive the importance of musical aptitude, manual dexterity, problem solving, creativity, and leadership, for examples, as important human conditions and ones that can be fostered successfully in classrooms. It is possible for the culturally disadvantaged child to be talented . . . gifted if you will. Yes, and it is also possible for these same children to be talented in areas in which, traditionally, we would not expect them to be talented, e.g., problem solving. These statements are far more than platitudes – they are realities! However, they demand teachers who are willing to avoid the common pitfalls of instruction. These teachers ignore debilitating labels. They apply positive reinforcement and do everything possible to fashion a more positive self-image on the part of the child. They circumvent the classic barrier to academic success – the inability to function effectively in reading. They attempt to communicate with the home and provide support there similar to that given at school.

The senior author recalls a seventh grade student under his jurisdiction who was termed "slow" and a "poor achiever". This seventh grader attended to these labels with care and expertise as he squandered his failure in math, social studies, and language arts. His same affective behaviors were destined to be tried in science class as well. The labels which were given to him by his teachers were accepted casually by himself and his peers. Further, these labels were also accepted by some of his teachers with considerable concern . . . even hostility. He was, in fact, quite capable of sending a select group of his teachers "up the classroom wall" at will. Still, the student had some characteristics that bent the patient teacher toward him. His smile at times was a winning smile and his sense of humor, although often misdirected, was keenly tuned. To attempt to proclaim that his science teacher had zero problems would be to falsify the issue but

science eventually proved to be the vehicle that ruined has academic
record of failure or near failure.

The key for this student proved to be a problem solving strategy that
directed the students to interact with the teacher in a manner that provided
the students with data leading toward closure with specific hypotheses.
This strategy demanded a good deal of divergent thinking on the parts of the
students prior to closure. This approach intrigued this young man because
he could think for himself and not be forced to read and regurgitate factual
information. It became evident that his ability to synthesize information
was extraordinary. Since the students were evaluated in a manner consistent
with the training, this young man earned an A in science. Remember, he was
labeled "slow" and a "poor achiever". And yet, his cognitive problem
solving ability was superb!

How many students like this one fail consistently and remain "slow"
or "failing" in classrooms across the nation? The number, unfortunately,
must be staggering and the prognosis for these young people is discouraging
at best unless we as educators meet their needs. You will undoubtedly
have that opportunity!

How Science Can
Provide Success
for a Broad Range
of Abilities!

The very nature of science is beautifully
structured to meeting the academic and
many of the general education needs of a
wide array of intellectual types. Surprisingly, there are few hard and fast,
right or wrong answers in science. Science, as you already know, is simply
man's way of empirically investigating his universe. This surely denotes a
continuum along which knowledge can be collected, i.e., empirical evidence
can range from minimal to exhaustive. Given any particular inquiry in the
classroom, therefore, children should be able to be successful in dealing
with it even though not all will function at the same level or with the same
expertise. Superficially, this may seem of only marginal significance.
But, when compared with the traditional format of "right" or "wrong", the
implications for academic success are staggering. Imagine an instructional
format which permits the teacher to positively reward all children. This
is precisely the potential of science - if taught as science and not simply
as a supplementary reading program. The same conditions, of course, should
exist in other curricular areas as well!

Let us use one example at this point to demonstrate this principle. If
in the intermediate grades, the teacher determines to focus on the "community
concept" in ecology, numerous inductive strategies are available. These
range from classroom investigations into microcommunities (e.g., those used
in the Science Curriculum Improvement Study) to investigations into locally
available macrocommunities (e.g., ponds and forests) or combinations of
these strategies or others. Assuming that the teacher uses an inductive
strategy which permits students to make their own observations and draw
their own conclusions, we can project a complex array of subconcepts being
generated from the investigations. One student might have the ability to
conceptualize the community at a very rudimentary level, e.g., the living

community is composed of plants and animals. Another may have the cognitive ability and motivation to generate a much more complex concept (or set of concepts, e.g., plants and animals in a living community interact and are interdependent. Further, some students may bring forth new inquiry possibilities, providing themselves with ways of extending their knowledge of the "community".

The diagram on the following page illustrates a few of the concepts and inquiry possibilities available from community investigation. Getting back to the original point, this helps demonstrate how science inquiry develops knowledge and new inquiry along a wide continuum and, therefore, has the potential for providing for a wide range of student abilities - from "slow" to "gifted".

Of course, one runs the risk of finding that teacher who demands all or nothing from his/her students. The "continuum strategy" would not work for a student under this teacher's leaderhip. This teacher, of course, manifests an inability to perceive the nature of man's cultural heritage and, in addition, fails to understand his/her responsibilities in a general education context. It is that same teacher who myopically expects all children to reach one level of human achievement and fails those who cannot. It is this same teacher who generally focuses on only a few facets of the human intellect in her classroom, generally the acquisition of factual information evaluted by true and false or poorly-constructed multiple choice tests. You, of course, can identify this teacher with little effort because he/she is the one who suffers from the "Johnny can't do that teachers' lounge syndrome". With better pre and inservice training, teachers with these characteristics are slowly disappearing from the American classroom. Unfortunately, no magic wand exists to instantaneously remove all such instruction from schools across the nation.

Hopefully, as you have been reading and thinking through this section, you have generated some logical thoughts about the kinds of activities appropriate for these kinds of students. Possibly, however, you have been waiting to be told of some appropriate strategies.

Earlier, you were given specific introduction to three of the major science programs in the United States, i.e., SAPA, ESS, and SCIS. Even though these programs differ markedly, each can be recommended for the purposes discussed in this section. Each is investigative in nature. Each permits at least some latitude in acceptable student progress. Each can be extended in terms of learning activities that go beyond the basic content provided by the program. None of the programs demands a great deal of reading skill in order for a child to succeed. Each program is based on the doing of science - a key characteristic for children who have hidden talents and a natural eagerness for investigating their environment. Further, each has been proven sound for a wide range of ability levels.

The teacher, however, need not use a major science program to provide for individual differences in the science area. The reader is directed to Part XIII of this worktext where attributes of an effective science program are listed. Any teacher who consistently plans for science instruction and

170

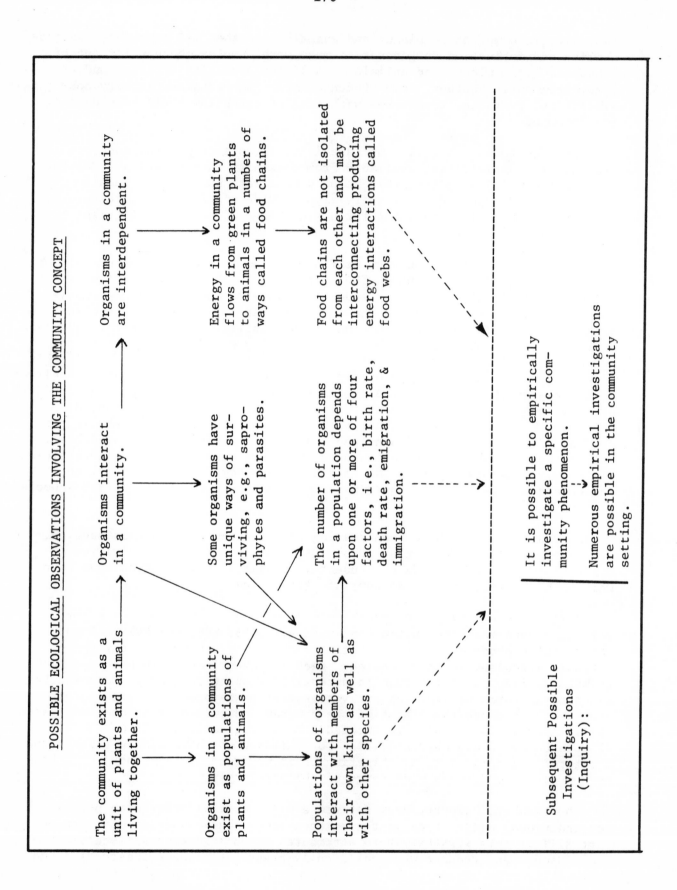

POSSIBLE ECOLOGICAL OBSERVATIONS INVOLVING THE COMMUNITY CONCEPT

The community exists as a unit of plants and animals living together.

Organisms in a community exist as populations of plants and animals.

Populations of organisms interact with members of their own kind as well as with other species.

Organisms interact in a community.

Some organisms have unique ways of surviving, e.g., saprophytes and parasites.

The number of organisms in a population depends upon one or more of four factors, i.e., birth rate, death rate, emigration, & immigration.

Organisms in a community are interdependent.

Energy in a community flows from green plants to animals in a number of ways called food chains.

Food chains are not isolated from each other and may be interconnecting producing energy interactions called food webs.

It is possible to empirically investigate a specific community phenomenon.

Numerous empirical investigations are possible in the community setting.

Subsequent Possible Investigations (Inquiry):

follows these principles and will be providing for a wide range of student ability.

Science for Disadvantaged Populations -   "Disadvantaged" is a relative term. Further, it should be used cautiously. It is, after all, another label and we have already discussed the debilitating effects of labels - both on teachers and students. Why, then use it here?

The writers choose to use the adjective simply to put the educational needs of differing populations in perspective and make suggestions in terms of using science as an effective tool in making greater numbers of human beings more effective members of society.

Perhaps the only generalization that is an absolute with reference to disadvantaged populations is that it is frighteningly difficult to generalize! There is no such thing as a typically disadvantaged human being, regardless of how many modifiers we use. One group of human beings may be culturally or educationally disadvantaged from one standpoint only to find another population disadvantaged from another. The poverty-stricken ghettoized black child is not the same individual as the midcontinent poverty-stricken and isolated white child. Neither of these conforms to the general description of the Mexican-American child caught up in the mores and cultural configurations of the migrant worker. And the impoverished Navajo child is different from all others. On and on . . .

Differing cultural patterns produce differing needs. Differing needs demand differing educational strategies and woe unto the teacher who finds representatives of two or more culturally deprived populations in the classroom. Indeed, the frustrations encountered in such a situation can be horrendous for the ethical teacher. Many teachers thusly challenged have seen fit to move or drop out of the education scene completely.

Still, we must begin somewhere and establish a premise for attacking the problem. What are the characteristics you might encounter in a given disadvantaged population of children?

Some Characteristics of the Disadvantaged Worthy of Note -   First, a culturally disadvantaged child is one who is kept, for one reason or another, from a wide variety of experiences which reflect the structure of the dominant culture. The child may be successful in the subculture in which he exists but almost totally incompetent to deal with those variables that permit success in standard educational programs and, subsequently, in the socio-economic cultural establishment in which he can find maximal fulfillment as a human being. Educational success is dependent, to a large extent, on the experiential backgrounds of the human beings involved and the disadvantaged child comes to a formal education quite often with a barren background, not knowing, for example, that the American reads from left to right and top to bottom.

A given disadvantaged population may also possess a system of values completely inconsistent with educational success. In fact, if there is one single detriment to success for many disadvantaged populations, this is it! The child perceives that his family cares not whether he succeeds in school. Further, and even worse, he overhears the routine four-letter criticisms leveled at teachers and schools. It becomes, then, not a matter of passive participation but one of overt aggression directed at any educational institution or human associated with that institution. Turning this situation around is excruciatingly difficult and this is one condition that must be countered if the disadvantaged child is to be culturally emancipated.

Self-image is still another criterion that creates educational problems. Consider the six or seven year old who perceives himself, to put it mildly, at less that standard and what do you have? You have a young human being who fails to believe in himself and, therefore, who is prone to failure. It is that simple!

And what of poverty? Can we generalize and state that economic deprivation is also one ingredient of cultural deprivation? Not necessarily! It is possible to be poor and culturally adjusted. It is possible to be wealthy and culturally maladjusted. Typically, however, there is a correlation between poverty and being culturally disadvantaged. Since the reasons appear obvious we won't go into them. But, to overgeneralize here is to glibly put labels on many children who don't deserve them - a tragedy that must be avoided if at all possible.

Can culturally disadvantaged children be perceived as individuals? Or, can this very category permit us to treat them all alike - for their own good? Even though the latter is sometimes done out of combinations of prejudice, sympathy, ignorance, fear, and misplaced benevolence, such must not be done. All children are individuals and all must be treated as individuals.

One of the very real dangers of labels is the stereotypes that follow the labels. All disadvantaged children, apart from being individuals, are disadvantaged by degrees. In fact, probably all human beings are disadvantaged to some degree. Further, where we turn the corner from "Culturally Advantaged Avenue" onto "Culturally Disadvantaged Avenue" is questionable. Generally, however, we would consider any child who lacks those values and experiential background that can afford success in school to be disadvantaged. Be that as it may, given ten disadvantaged children, you probably have ten different degrees of disadvantagedness.

What Can We Do For
the Disadvantaged?

We begin on a note of pessimism. The writer's own educational background, working with ghettoized blacks and urban disadvantaged whites as well as rurally disadvantaged children, demands a straightforward cautionary note. For those young people who come to the educational experience with a set of values not commensurate with the values espoused by basic educational institutions (i.e., that education is a productive and worthwhile endeavor), some strategy must be embraced that can modify those debilitating values. If the inappropriate values cannot be changed, any other efforts to improve the students' education experience will be largely worthless. As tragic as it appears, this tends to be reality. Further, if the debilitating values are reinforced over and over again at home, efforts to change those values via a school-centered experience are fraught with failure. Can nothing be done? On the contrary, a great deal can be done but only where a method exists to help modify values communicated by the home.

What strategies work? None work completely. However, if the school or its agent can help the parent(s) perceive the value that an education can have for the child, the values communicated to the child in the home can change and the child's attitude toward school effectively modified. Some schools have a visiting counselor program to facilitate change. Some schools rely on the teacher to go into the home and help establish a positive relationship. A variety of strategies can be employed. However, the attempt must be made!

With respect to the child's self-image, the teacher can do a great deal. One effective strategy is to employ a cycle of success for the child - to structure the educational world so as to permit the child to enjoy and experience success over time. Once a decent self-image begins to appear, a belief in "self" contributes to academic effort and achievement. As noted in a prior paragraph, science offers great potential here because it can lead to success at various levels of cognitive performance.

The easiest problem with which to deal (and one where many schools fail miserably) is that related to the child's experiential background. The disadvantaged child needs an expanded experiential base from which he can operate intellectually. Further, these experiences should be acquired in contact with the real, three-dimensional world of the child. One of the major failures of the elementary school is its seeming psychosis for keeping children within the confines of two book covers and four classroom walls. This basic absurdity disregards almost completely the realities of the environment in which the disadvantaged child exists and assumes that a totally surrogate world can meet the educational and social needs of such a child.

Answers are not absolute but many suggestions can be given which effectively deal with the child's experiential awareness. First, and foremost, experiences should be concrete, particularly for young children. An opportunity to manipulate the three-dimensional world is crucial for effective conceptualization. The closer the experience is to reality, the better the intellectual pegs on which the child can hang his memory. Instead of reading about how bicycles produce a mechanical advantage, why not bring one into the classroom and study gear ratios in reality? And yet, how often is this done? Instead of reading about and seeing pictures of trees and their ecological roles, why not have each child choose a tree or shrub in the area and observe it on a select schedule so that a log or diary of observations can be maintained? And, yet, it is doubtful that many teachers of disadvantaged children use the "Tree Diary" as a means of extending knowledge. Instead of talking about seasonal change, why not take a field trip to observe change - to measure the length of shadows as they change over time - and observe the relationship that exists between the position of the sun and seasons?

The writers believe, also, that a regular, experiential science program can effectively promote science and, therefore, cultural awareness. However, for the disadvantaged child this is probably not enough. You may question this position because you know how much time must be spent on the basic skills. There is really no time for science? Or the social studies? Too much time has to be spent on the 3 R's? But, the 3 R's are of little worth to the disadvantaged child when treated out of the context of reality. This is one reason why many efforts for providing for culturally disadvantaged children have failed. Some teachers unfortunately perceive skills as an end in themselves and the content leading to those skills to be insignificant. In actuality, the reverse is the appropriate perception! Use content that turns the child on! Use content that the child needs! Use those content selections as vehicles to get at skills! This works surprisingly well.

It then becomes a problem of providing more science experiences (or environmental experiences if you prefer) for the disadvantaged child than for the "advantaged" youngster. When the content portion of the curriculum provides for both conceptual awareness and for vehicles to get at basic skills, this problem becomes negligible. This pattern provides the time needed.

One of the major thrusts of education for the disadvantaged child has been to deal with the child's own environment, i.e., use the child's own setting as a focus for educational experiences. If in an urban setting and studying insects, one would deal with the cockroaches, flies, lice, and bed bugs of the ghetto. If studying mammals, he would deal with feral dogs and cats, gerbils, rats, and other human beings. If studying food chains, he would explore the food chains in which sparrows, chimney swifts, cockroaches, rats, lice and bed bugs were involved. This strategy has its merits because the child has already established referents to many of these objects. It is entirely true that familiarity breeds success. However, the educational program dare not end there. Eventually, the disadvantaged child must be taken out of his immediate environment. The rationale is so simple that it boggles the mind to see educators who fail to perceive it. If we do not expand the cultural horizons of the disadvantaged, we simply provide a condition that guarantees that the child cannot escape his subcultural destiny. To do so is educationally unethical. Many are the urban children who have absolutely no concept of "country". Many are the rural children who have little concept of "city" or "subway". Both populations may never have been to a zoo or a planetarium much less a seashore or a museum.

The implications are clear. These children must be taken out of the classroom and exposed to segments of their universe with which they have had no contact and with which they need contact. And yet, the writers have met potentially competent teachers who refuse to leave the classroom even when they have the opportunity. Similarly, there are teachers who would love to use the real, three-dimensional world to expand cultural horizons only to be refused that opportunity by their administrators and/or school boards.

In either situation, it is critical to change the conditions - for children who desperately need expanded horizons.

In Summary   It can be debilitating to put labels on
                                    children in classrooms even though
categorization is sometimes necessary before remediation can take place.
To identify children as "slow" or "gifted" on the basis of I.Q. and reading
ability is to refuse to accept many of the talents and potential talents
of children. Science, because of its openended nature, is adaptable to a
wide assortment of children with differing needs and abilities. Science
instruction can provide a vehicle whereby all children can enjoy success
and still allow for the "gifted" child.

Numerous cultural variables impede scholastic success for the "disadvantaged" student. Students' values and self-images must be commensurate
with educational values and a belief in one's self before major achievement
can occur. A broad experiential background is essential for educational
success. If appropriate steps are taken, a child's experiential background
can be strengthened substantially by the school. Science provides an
excellent vehicle for broadening experiential backgrounds and providing for
training in basic skills in other content areas. Although it is essential
to use the disadvantaged child's environmental frame of reference as an
educational tool, his cultural referents must also be increased in order
to provide for an expanding foundation for personal success.

Food for Thought

There may be other things which schools could or
should do, but they could or should do these
things only after they have, . . ., patiently and
persistently as they can, taught the use of that
unique instrument of their humanity, the restless,
questing mind. . . . Whenever a boy or girl in this
country receives a less challenging, less appropriate, less worthy education than he or she
mentally and morally deserves, there is a diminishing
of the person, an impoverishing of a life, possibly
a great loss to the nation, and a defeat suffered
in the sector of the engagement of the mind of man
with the mystery and wonder of the universe.

William H. Cornog - 1963

176

PART XIII

A Comparison of Traditional and Modern Science Methods

TRADITIONAL SCIENCE METHODS

STUDENTS:

- READ AND MEMORIZE
    information about science
- AND DO
    cookbook lab exercises
- WHICH REFLECT
    little motivation
- IN ORDER TO
    please the teacher
    gain a good grade
- WHICH RESULTS IN
    poor retention
    little transfer
    few cognitive skills
    failure for many
- AND DEVELOPING THE ATTITUDE THAT
    education is boring
- AND EXPERIENCE
    a poor educational technology.

MODERN SCIENCE METHODS

STUDENTS:

- PARTICIPATE IN
    the science enterprise
- WITH
    high motivation
- BECAUSE THEY ARE
    doing science
- WHICH RESULTS IN
    inductively derived concepts
    cognitive skills – processes
    long term retention
    transfer potential
    success for many
- AND DEVELOPING THE ATTITUDE THAT
    school might be an exciting
        place to be
- AND EXPERIENCE
    an improving educational technology.

CONDITIONS NECESSARY FOR AN EFFECTIVE ELEMENTARY SCHOOL SCIENCE PROGRAM

1. The science program should be considered as an integral part of the general education of all children in that it focuses on the development of scientifically literate human beings.

2. Adequate time should be provided for the science program; no less that 150 minutes per week should be scheduled for science. Further, teachers should recognize the value of science as a content vehicle in a number of other curricular areas and wisely use it for that purpose.

3. The science program should continually be evaluated in terms of whether it is meeting its goals and, in particular, the general education needs of children.

4. The science program should teach both cognitive skills (science process) and important conceptual knowledge. Further, these same skills and concepts must be taught in such a way as to permit their transfer to new and unique situations of importance to the students.

5. The science program should be experientially oriented whenever possible. Students must have an opportunity to DO SCIENCE.

6. The science program should develop in each child a concept of what science is and what kind of a human being a scientist is.

7. The science program should provide for a wide distribution of student abilities, i.e., all students should be successful in meeting instructional objectives in science.

8. The science program should reflect specific instructional objectives and these objectives should be communicated to the students and used for evaluation.

9. The science program should provide students with a set of attitudes toward their natural world and toward science commensurate with their personal needs and the needs of the society in which they live.

   A. The science program should provide a concept of the tremendous implications science has had on society as well as a correct concept which alludes to the very real limitations of science as they pertain to solving many of man's personal and social problems.

B. The science program should help the child understand that he is inexorably tied to his environment and that his survival and the survival of subsequent generations depends upon man's management of that same environment.

10. The science program should incorporate not only the intellectual facets of pure science but also the domain of technology in order that every student can differentiate between science and technology and also understand the relationship that exists between them.

. . . demand that every citizen have a basic and functional understanding of the products of science - the concepts, the principles and the facts; and be able to understand and use the process of science - the modes of thought, the attitudes of mind, the tactics and strategy, and the appreciations.. . . This goal can be achieved through the schools in every hamlet and city across the Nation. It can be realized, how- ever, only as it is initiated by local effort and grows up from the grass roots. It must have the support of every citizen in every local community. It will require a concerted and organized effort, but these costs are low when weighed against the realization that this kind of education in science may be basic to our survival.

Ellsworth S. Obourn - 1961

APPENDICES

APPENDIX A

Twig Model and Twig Drawings for Classification

Fig. 1

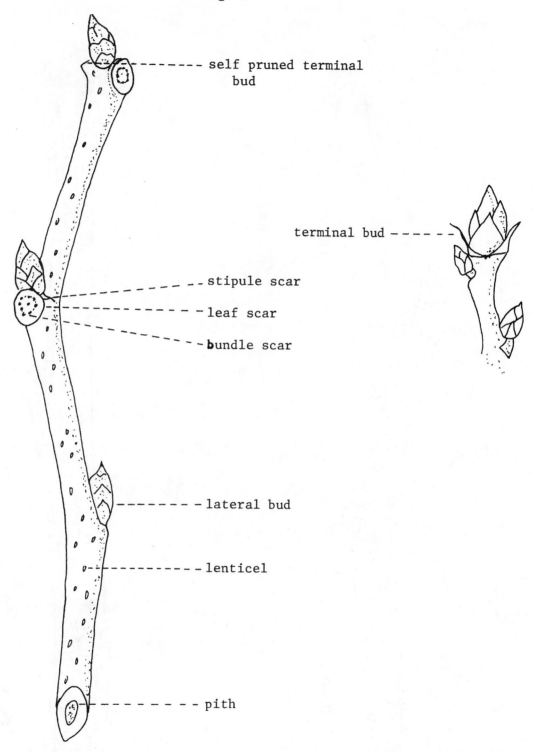

self pruned terminal
bud

terminal bud -----

stipule scar

leaf scar

bundle scar

lateral bud

lenticel

pith

Typical Winter Twig Characters

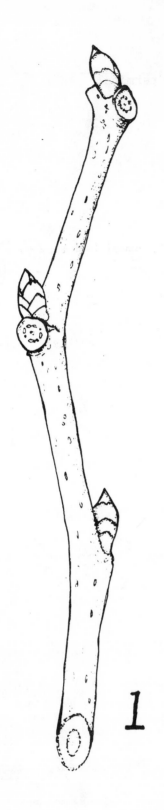

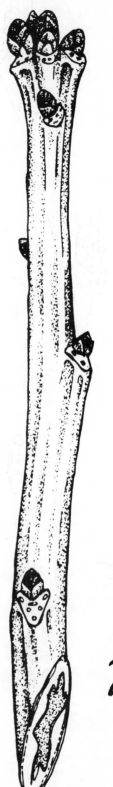

1

2

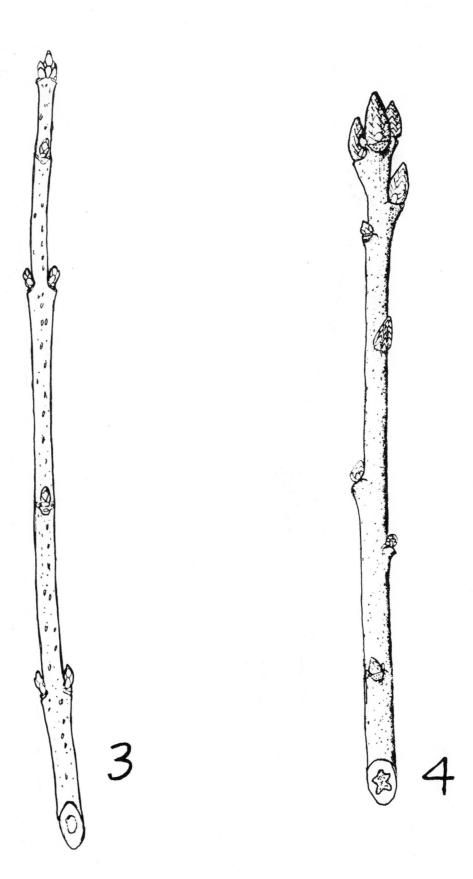

3

4

5

6

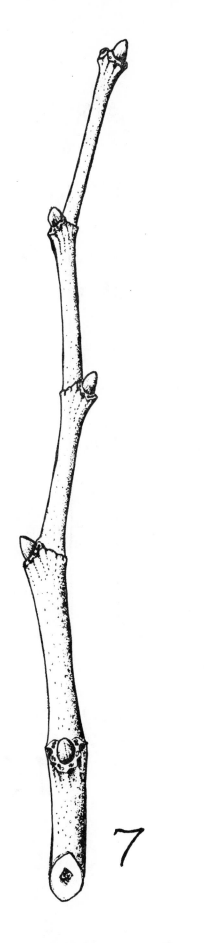

7

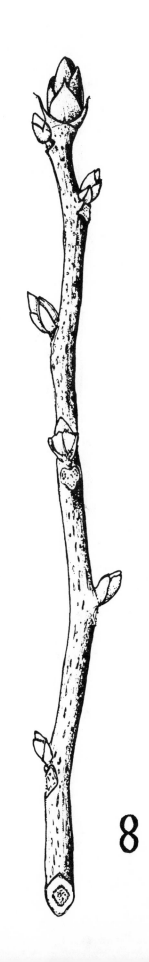

8

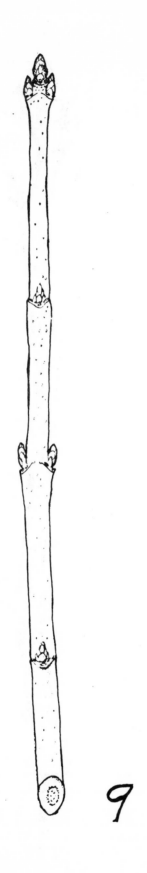

9

10

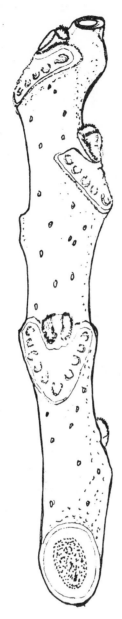

11

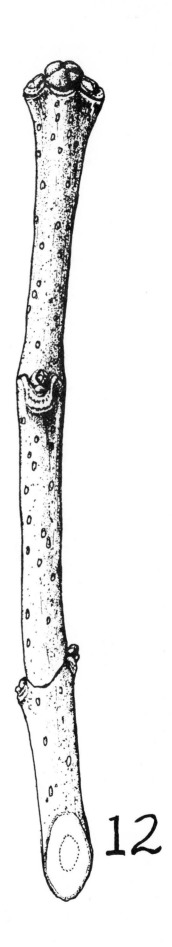

12

APPENDIX B

Textbook Appraisal

Textbook Appraisal

Your Name _____ Date _____

Publisher _____ Pub. Date _____

Grade Level Chosen _____ I. Certain science <u>content</u> is represented in particular chapters or units in every text, e.g., botany, geology, earth science. Below, check all content areas represented by chapters (or units) in the text with which you are working. Write the unit headings or chapter titles encompassed by these content areas in the column to the right.

<u>Content</u>   <u>Chapter or Unit Headings</u>

_____ Chemistry

_____ Physics

_____ Earth Science, The Atmosphere

_____ Earth Science, Geology

_____ Earth Science, Oceanography

_____ General Botany

_____ General Zoology

_____ Anatomy

_____ Ecology

_____ Environmental Problems

_____ The Nature of Science

_____ Other _____

_____ Other _____

_____ Other _____

_____ Other _____

II. Many textbook publishers use a "sprial approach" to science content, repeating the same content two or more times in a series of different conceptual levels as students develop. Are the same content areas noted on the previous page covered in other texts in this series of· science books?

Yes _____ No _____   Evidence for your response:

III. Are content areas covered that teach important conceptual knowledge that students cannot learn by first-hand experiences with objects and events in the environment, e.g., the solar system, space travel, biogeography, oceanography.

Yes _____ No _____   If yes, what is the evidence?

IV. Is the text a health/science fusion, i.e., does it cover mental and/or physical health as a basic part of science? (Please do not consider the study of anatomy and physiology per se as evidence of health instruction.) Note: Be sure you refer to the entire series in responding to this question.

Yes _____ No _____ If yes, what is the evidence?

V. Questions are asked of students in any science text. They are found
interspersed within chapters or at a special section at the end of the chapter
or both. Please study the manner in which the authors have structured
these questions. Respond to the following assignments:

A. Are there questions measuring the acquisition of factual information?
(Model: What is the food-making process in plants called?) Yes _____ No _____

Example:

B. Are there questions that measure the acquisition of conceptual knowledge?
(Model: How does a lever work?) Yes _____ No _____

Example:

C. Are there questions that also measure the student's ability to apply
newly acquired information? (Model: If the earth is rotating in space,
why are we not thrown off its surface?)

Example:

VI. Most texts claim that they are activity (experientially) oriented. These
activities, oftentimes called experiments or investigations, are also found
interspersed within chapters or units or at a special section at the end of
the chapter or both. Carefully examine the manner in which the authors have
developed several of these activities. Then, respond to the following
assignments:

A. Are the activities primarily structured to have the child inductively form
a concept or are they structured to deductively demonstrate an already
pre-stated concept?

Your conclusion with example(s):

B. Are the activities developed so that there is an opportunity for open-ended
independent investigation or must the child follow a prescribed sequence of
events which lead to a predetermined answer?

Your conclusion with example(s):

C. In your opinion, do the activities seem to have general education significance for children, i.e., will the activities enable the child to become a more effective member of his society?

Yes _____ No _____ Why do you respond as you do?

VII. A. Is there any evidence in the student text to indicate that students gain a concept of what science is? This could be accomplished with a direct definition, discussion or repeated reference to science. Although a child might gain this concept inductively, by experiencing science in a realistic manner, your instructor must perceive an adequate explanation if you use this perspective in your reasoning.

Yes _____ No _____ If yes, what is the evidence?

VII. B. (Respond here only if you had to answer "No" to the preceding question.) If there is no evidence that students get an explanation of what science is, might there be an explanation given in the teacher's guide in a manner that could be communicated to the students?

Yes _____ No _____ If yes, what is the evidence?

VIII. In terms of your perception of the importance of technology, do you
feel that the technological applications of science are adequately treated
in this textbook? (Technology refers to man's cultural application of science
knowledge, e.g., communications, space travel, surface transportation, tools.)

Yes _____ No _____ Evidence pro or con:

IX. A. Is there any evidence in the text to indicate that students get
experience with or training in specific science skills (processes) e.g.,
hypothesizing, comparing, classifying, predicting, experimenting?

Yes _____ No _____ If yes, evidence:

IX. B. If skills are developed as a part of the science program, are students
evaluated in their ability to use these intellectual processes rather than
being evaluated for the acquisition of facts and/or concepts?

Yes _____ No _____ Evidence either way:

X. Are students taught what scientific attitudes are, e.g., the value of suspending judgment in scientific investigation and/or the attitude that reliable science information is obtained only after much research and data collection?

Yes _____ No _____ Evidence either way:

XI. Most textbook publishers make a point of noting that a particular text develops important concepts. Choose any one specific concept from anywhere in the text, state the concept below, and continue with this part of the assignment as directed below: (Model concept: Energy is exchanged in the environment through food chains beginning with the food producing green plant.)

Write the chosen
concept in this
space:

A. What printed information and/or illustrations are found in the text which would help the child develop this particular concept?

B. What science experiences (laboratory or otherwise) do students get with regard to this particular concept? In other words, what do students DO to help them develop this concept?

C. What suggestions are there in the <u>Teacher's</u> <u>Edition</u> for the development of this concept?

D. Do A, B, and C. above provide enough <u>information</u> and <u>experience</u> to permit the thorough development of this concept? Defend your answer! Think it through carefully!!

Yes _____ No _____ Defense:

XII. Are various kinds of illustrations used to good advantage in this series? Consider how line drawings, full color art work, and full color photographs implement learning for the child. Comment using specific examples.

Yes _____ No _____ Comment:

XIII. Please assume that, for one reason or another, you <u>had</u> <u>to</u> <u>use</u> this textbook series in your own classroom as the basic science program. With this in mind, please do the following:

A. List what you perceive as the strengths, if any, of the series.

B. List what you perceive as the weaknesses, if any, of the series.

C. Prepare a detailed explanation of how you would use this series, modify it, or supplement it in order to gain the best possible science experiences for your students. In other words, how would you use this series to provide for scientific literacy on the parts of your students? Please be very specific in your presentation. Use the reverse side of this sheet to complete this part of the assignment.

APPENDIX C

More On Concepts - - An Assignment

More On Concepts - - An Assignment

As you now know, conceptual knowledge is the basis for what we know and, further, provides an intellectual foundation which permits us to mediate new information. To a marked degree, conceptual knowledge also assists us in the use of the skills of critical thinking, i.e., the scientific processes.

Every intellectual discipline of man (e.g., history, sociology, biology, chemistry and earth science) has a certain conceptual or cognitive structure. It is this structure that permits the domain of that discipline to be inter-preted and made available to us intellectually. The bulk of the structure of the knowledge of any discipline is conceptual in nature.

Permit us an example of a small compartment of the structure of the con-ceptual knowledge in one intellectual discipline, earth science. All of us know that the landscape features on the earth's surface make up the physio-graphy of this planet. Let us start there and further clarify the "why" of physiography using a set of closely related concepts. See if you see the relationships between these concepts:

> Concept 1. Both naturally occurring constructive and destructive forces influence the development of landscape features on the earth's surface.

> Concept 2. Naturally occurring <u>constructive</u> forces include volcanism and diastrophism, i.e., the bending or breaking of rocks in the earth's crust.

> Concept 3. Naturally occurring <u>destructive</u> forces include those factors involved in the weathering or breaking up of rocks (e.g., solution, frost wedging, exfoliation) plus those factors involved in the erosion or transportation of rock debris (e.g., gravity, wind, water).

Now, we could go on from this point and further develop each major concept stated above but that shouldn't be necessary. You should see the relationships existing between these concepts and perceive why a person's understanding of these would be dependent upon his background of experiences with the objects and phenomena described by those conceptual statements.

Now, there appear to be a couple of things that are important here for teachers of children. Without arguing the points we will arbitrarily state that: (1) Before teachers can effectively provide meaningful learning experiences for students they must have some understanding of the structure of the knowledge with which they are dealing; (2) Teachers who have the option of deciding what is to be taught should make decisions based on the impor-tance of the information to the child. That is, <u>what</u> is truly important from a general education point of view: This correctly infers that we <u>must</u> be able to defend what we teach.

If one were to teach the three concepts above dealing with the changing earth's surface, he might logically use the following defense for his position"

> Rationale: Man is an inhabitant of the planet earth and, so far at least, is bound to the planet and dependent on it for his very survival. It is quite clear that the interactions between man and his environment are numerous and include those that take place with the earth's crust.
>
> Although many of the forces of crustal construction and destruction are subtle in nature, several are dynamic and dramatic, e.g., volcanoes, earthquakes, landslides. An understanding of the nature of crustal movement and change should help facilitate a human's adjustment to his environment (this would, of course, include freedom from fear and superstition).
>
> Further, the factors of weathering and erosion are of critical importance to man's personal welfare in that weathering substantially contributes to soil formation and the forces of erosion can wreak havoc with man's agricultural lands. Similarly, exercising control over the environment (with respect to weathering and erosion) demands that man first understand the phenomena he is attempting to control. It would appear, then, that the culturally applicable aspects of these concepts hold considerable promise for improving man's relationship with the universe in which he lives.

The Assignment — Because your professors perceive the logical decision-making related to science content to be crucial to a fundamentally sound science program they are going to give you an opportunity to get involved in this endeavor.

This involvement will include the judicial selection of conceptual knowledge and a reasonable and logical defense for that selection. You are to prepare a two page paper following the task descriptions below:

Task One: Choose a portion of a science discipline and prepare a set of related conceptual statements which you perceive to be of critical importance to human beings. This concept set should consist of no fewer than two and no more than four.

Task Two: You have chosen the related concepts! Now, tell us what gives you the right to take up the child's time and energy in the development or acquisition of these concepts. Why are these concepts important — or crucial — to a human being's general education? State a logical and meaningful rationale using no more than 200 words. Be as succinct as possible!

APPENDIX D

Responses for Pros, Cons, and A Lesson on Behavioral Objectives

Performance Terms:

1. select, (define)*; 2. write, (hypothesize)*; 3. write (design)*;
4. classify; 5. inspect, repair; 6. compare, state. (* = performance
terms that are inferred in the individual statements, e.g., in No. 2, the
student is asked to write a hypothesis so the inferred task is hypothesizing.
The student is not asked to experiment in No. 2 so experimentation would not
be a performance term in No. 2.)

Are They Behaviorally Stated?   (Model Responses)

3. The student will prepare a written statement, not to exceed 50 words,
which describes the relationship between work and energy.

4. The student will present a 10 minute oral report which partially explains
the importance of soil, water, forest, and wildlife resources. Subsequently,
he will state one way in which he can successfully participate in the conservation of at least three of these resources.

Applying What You Have Learned: (Model responses)

1. Asked whether his shadow is longer at 2:00 PM on Sept. 22 or on Nov. 22,
the student will respond with the correct answer.
     Asked if his home town or school gets more light energy from the sun in
October or November, the student will respond with the correct answer.
Subsequently, when asked it it gets colder or warmer from September to
December, he will respond correctly.

2. Following the lesson on energy exchanges in the biosphere, the student
will be able to . . . (a) . . . select the right response in a multiple
choice test item which explains that photosynthesis is the process whereby
green plants manufacture food. (b) . . . orally state the names of the two
compounds which are chemically combined in the presence of chlorophyll and
light energy when carbohydrates are being produced by a green plant. (c)
. . . write a sentence of no more than 20 words explaining the relationship
between photosynthesis and food energy in the biosphere.

3. Following the unit on soil conservation the student will, given a sheet
of paper on which five soil conservation problems are listed and five control
measures listed, be able to orally state where three of each of these were
observed during the field trip.

4. Following the instruction on food chains and food webs the student will be
able to construct a simple diagram of a food chain (minimum of three steps)
and a diagram of a food web (showing relationships of at least three organisms
in a food web), label each organism as to whether it's a producer, first-order
consumer, etc., and state in writing which diagram is the food chain and which is
the food web.

APPENDIX E

Metric Measure

Metric Measure

<u>Temperature:</u>

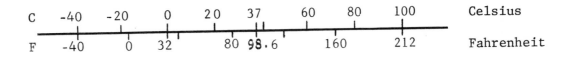

To obtain a Celsius temperature merely subtract 32 from the Fahrenheit
temperature. Take 5/9 of that figure. Example:

```
  212 F
-  32
  180 X 5/9 = 100 C.
```

To obtain a Fahrenheit temperature merely multiply the Celsius temperature
by 9/5. Add 32 to this figure. This yields Fahrenheit temperature. Example:

```
37 C X 9/5 = 66.6
           + 32.0
             98.6 F
```

<u>Weight</u> (<u>Mass</u>):

1 ounce	=	28 grams (g)
1 pound	=	0.45 kilograms (kg)
1 ton (2000 lb)	=	0.9 tonnes (t)

* * * * * *

1 gram (g)	=	0.035 ounces
1 kilogram (kg)	=	2.2 pounds
1 tonne (1000 kg)	=	1.1 tons

Linear Measure:

Approximate conversions both ways . . .

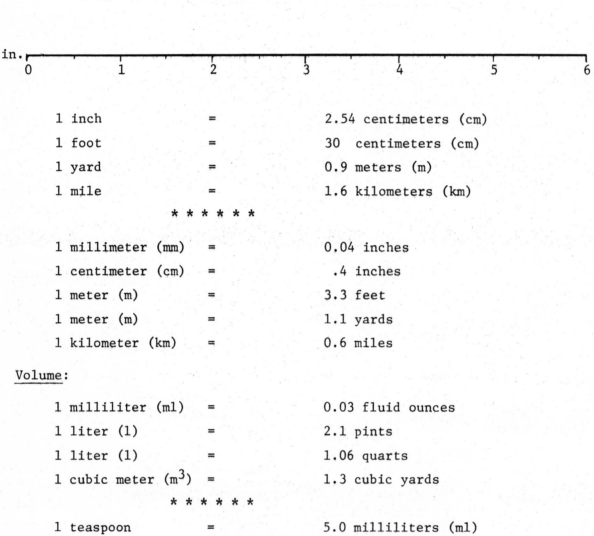

1 inch	=	2.54 centimeters (cm)
1 foot	=	30 centimeters (cm)
1 yard	=	0.9 meters (m)
1 mile	=	1.6 kilometers (km)

* * * * * *

1 millimeter (mm)	=	0.04 inches
1 centimeter (cm)	=	.4 inches
1 meter (m)	=	3.3 feet
1 meter (m)	=	1.1 yards
1 kilometer (km)	=	0.6 miles

Volume:

1 milliliter (ml)	=	0.03 fluid ounces
1 liter (1)	=	2.1 pints
1 liter (1)	=	1.06 quarts
1 cubic meter (m^3)	=	1.3 cubic yards

* * * * * *

1 teaspoon	=	5.0 milliliters (ml)
1 tablespoon	=	15.0 milliliters (ml)
1 ounce	=	30.0 milliliters (ml)
1 pint	=	0.47 liters (1)
1 cubic yard	=	0.76 cubic meters (m^3)

APPENDIX F

Supplementary Reading Assignment

Supplementary Reading Assignment

This assignment is designed to broaden your background in a facet of elementary school science education which is of particular concern to YOU. The number of required readings plus continued reading (done on your own hopefully) will keep you abreast of current thinking in the field. The assignment is meant to be an opportunity to give you an in-depth view of the topic you choose.

INSTRUCTIONS:

1. You will choose a topic in elementary science education, either from the suggested list found below or one of your own interest, which requires the agreement of your instructor. Samples of topics are: 1) discovery learning in science; 2) the unit approach to science education; 3) the developmental science curriculum; 4) programmed learning in science; 5) science for the gifted child; 6) TV science instruction; 7) developing scientific attitudes; 8) the use of behavioral objectives in science; 9) incidental science experiences; 10) motivation in science; 11) using community resources in science; 12) multidisciplinary science; 13) the role of outdoor education in science; 14) environmental education; 15) the textbook and its place in science education; 16) concept development in science; 17) the use of science with special populations; and 18) using science in special education.

2. You will then read at least SIX (6) journal articles on your chosen topic. Please select a topic on which you can find sufficient, current journal coverage (1965 to present). SUGGESTED JOURNALS ARE:

Science and Children   School Science and Mathematics
The Science Teacher   Science Education
The American Biology Teacher   Journal of Research in Science Teaching

Also use the Reader's Guide and the Education Index. Pertinent articles often appear in such journals as Illinois Education; NEA Journal (Today's Education; the Instructor; Teacher and others. Please be sure that the articles you choose directly relate to your topic.

3. After reading these articles you will prepare a 500 word paper (maximum) which is to be a synopsis of the topic on which you have become knowledgeable. This is not to be a discussion of the six separate articles. Use the ideas gleaned from your articles in your discussion of the topic. You should also evaluate the information read in the articles as part of the paper's coverage.

4. The end produce (paper) is to be a typewritten, concise, coherent, smooth-flowing synopsis of the topic you selected. The paper will include:

a. a title page designating your topic and identifying your authorship

b. the paper itself (watch your word limits -- 500!)

c. citations within the paper (incorporated into your synopsis) of some of the bibliographical references you used. A good way is to use the name of the author of the article if you paraphrase or quote from your references. PLEASE DO NOT USE FOOTNOTES.

d. a final paragraph containing YOUR HONEST EVALUATION of the ideas you have presented in this paper. Platitudes and glittering generalities are not appreciated.

e. a bibliography (on a separate sheet of paper) of the articles you used (READ) to gather information for your topic. Your bibliography must include AT LEAST TWO DIFFERENT journals within the six you have listed. The bibliography is to be done in a standard, correct style. One such example is presented below:

Williams, David L. "On Science for Young Children." Science and Children 13: 34-35; October 1975.

5. DUE DATE: As announced by your instructor.

6. GRADING: Your grade will be based on the degree to which your paper has met the guidelines of this assignment. The following criteria will be used:

a. organization and discussion of the topic

b. cited use of references in the paper

c. bibliography (relevancy of articles, diversity of journals, correct form)

d. summary - your evaluation of the topic covered (quality and depth of perception)

APPENDIX G

Resources and References for Elementary School Science Teachers

Resources and References for Elementary School Science Teachers

Several of the problems of the elementary school science teacher are those of "where do I look for . . ?" or "how do I do this . . .?" or better yet, "what can I do, activity-wise to teach science well?". Another problem is a concern for how to tool oneself in science content and ancillary methods so that a teacher can himself cope with the broad spectrum of scientific knowledge before he teaches it. Your instructors have compiled the following listings to provide you with information sources as at least a beginning solution to the problems stated above.

PUBLISHERS

Addison-Wesley Publishing Co.
Reading, Massachusetts 01867
(textbook publisher)

American Book Company
300 Pike Street
Cincinnati, Ohio 45202
(textbook publisher)

Commission on Science Education
American Association for the
Advancement of Science
1515 Massachusetts Ave., N. W.
Washington, D. C. 20005
(materials on science education
in general as well as the
Science: A Process Approach
program)

The Bobbs-Merrill Co., Inc.
4300 West 62nd Street
Indiannapolis, Ind. 46206
(textbook publisher)

Childrens Press, Inc.
1224 West Van Buren St.
Chicago, Illinois 60607
(supplementary science books
for children)

Follett Publishing Co.
1010 W. Washington Blvd.
Chicago, Illinois 60607
(textbook publisher - science
and sex education)

Ginn and Company
Statler Building
Back Bay P. O. 191
Boston, Massachusetts 02117
(textbook publisher)

Golden Press, Inc.
(Education Division)
850 Third Avenue
New York, N. Y. 10016
(supplemental science content
books for children)

Harcourt, Brace and Jovanovich
757 Third Avenue
New York, N. Y. 10016
(textbook publisher)

Harper and Row Publishers
49 East 33rd Street
New York, N. Y.
(textbook publisher)

D. C. Heath and Co.
2700 N. Richardt Ave.
Indiannapolis, Ind. 46219
(textbook publisher)

Holt, Rinehart & Winston, Inc.
373 Madison Aveneue
New York, N. Y. 10017
(textbook publisher)

Houghton Mifflin Company
53 West 43rd Street
New York, N. Y. 10036
(textbook publisher)

Laidlaw Brothers
Thatcher and Madison Sts.
River Forest, Illinois 60305
(textbook publisher)

The MacMillan Company
866 Third Aveneue
New York, N. Y. 10022
(textbook publisher)

McGraw Hill Book Company
Webster Publishing Division
Manchester Road
Manchester, Missouri 63011
(textbook publisher and
distributor of Elementary
Science Study materials)

National Science Teachers Assoc.
1201 16th Street
Washington, D. C. 20036
(elementary science journals
and supplementary teaching
aids)

Rand McNally and Company
P. O. Box 7600
Chicago, Illinois 60680
(resource and textbooks,
SCIS materials)

Scott Foresman and Company
1900 East Lake Avenue
Glenview, Illinois 60025
(textbook publisher)

Silver Burdett Company
P. O. Box 362
Morriston, New Jersey 07960
(textbook publisher)

J. Weston Walch, Publisher
919 Congress Street
Portland, Maine 04104
(resource guides, slides and
poster sets, worktexts, etc.)

Xerox Education Division
600 Madison Avenue
New York, N. Y. 10022
(materials for Science: A
Process Approach program)

AUDIO-VISUAL AID PRODUCERS

AV-ED Productions
7939 Santa Monica Blvd.
Hollywood, California 90046

Canadian National Film Board
1271 Avenue of the Americas
New York, N. Y. 10020

Churchill Films
662 N. Robertson Blvd.
Los Angeles, California 90069

Coronet Instructional Films
65 E. South Water Street
Chicago, Illinois 60601

Eye Gate House
146-01 Archer Avenue
Jamaica, N. Y. 11435

Film Associates
1159 Santa Monica Blvd.
Los Angeles, California 90025

Jam Handy Organization
2821 E. Grand Blvd.
Detroit, Michigan 48211

Indiana University
Audio-Visual Center
Bloomington, Indiana

McGraw Hill Films
330 West 42nd Street
New York, N. Y. 10036

Society for Visual Education, Inc.
1345 West Diversey Parkway
Chicago, Illinois 60614

U. S. Department of Agriculture
Motion Picture Services
Washington, D. C. 20250

EQUIPMENT AND SUPPLY DISTRIBUTORS

American Optical Company
Box A
Buffalo, N. Y. 14215
(microscopes and other
optical instruments)

Bausch and Lomb Inc.
635 St. Paul Street
Rochester, N. Y. 14602
(microscopes and other
optical instruments)

Bioscope Manufacturing Co.
P. O. Box 1492
Tulsa, Oklahoma 74101
(microprojector)

Carolina Biological Supply Co.
Burlington, North Carolina 27215
(general science equipment
and materials)

Central Scientific Company
1700 Irving Park
Chicago, Illinois 60613
(general science supplies
and equipment)

Denoyer-Geppert Company
5235 Ravenswood Ave.
Chicago, Illinois 60640
(charts, models, transparencies)

General Biological Supply House
8200 South Hoyne Avenue
Chicago, Illinois 60620
(living and non-living materials)

Graf-Apsco Company
5868 Broadway
Chicago, Illinos
(microscopes and other
optical equipment)

Jewel Aquarium Company, Inc.
5005 West Armitage Avenue
Chicago, Illinois 60639
(aquaria and allied supplies)

Ken-A-Vision Manufacturing Co., Inc.
5615 Raytown Road
Raytown, Missouri 64133
(microprojectors)

Macalaster Scientific Corp.
60 Arsenal Street
Watertown, Massachusetts 02172
(general science equipment and supplies)

A. J. Nystrom & Company
3333 Elston Avenue
Chicago, Illinois 60618
(maps, globes, charts, models)

Ohaus Scale Corporation
1050 Commerce Avenue
Union, New Jersey 07083
(laboratory balances - all levels)

Science Kit, Inc.
2299 Military Road
Tonawanda, N. Y. 14140
(general science supplies and equipment)

Trippensee Planetarium Co., Inc.
2200 South Hamilton Street
Saginaw, Michigan 48602
(models, globes and charts)

Ward's Natural Science Establishment, Inc.
3000 Ridge Road East
P. O. Box 1712
Rochester, N. Y. 14603
(materials for earth science and biology)

W. Atlee Burpee Company
Philadelphia, Pennsylvania 19132
(seeds, bulbs, plants)

CONTENT AND METHODS REFERENCE BOOKS FOR TEACHERS

General Methods Books:

Elementary School Science and How to Teach It
by
Glenn Blough and Julius Schwarts
Holt, Rinehart and Winston (publishers)

A Sourcebook for Elementary Science
by
Paul F. Brandwein, Editor
Harcourt Brace and Jovanovich, Inc. (publishers

Science Activities . . . for Elementary Children
by
Nelson and Lorbeer
Wm. C. Brown Company Publishers
135 S. Locust Street
Dubuque, Iowa   52002

Guppies, Bubbles and Vibrating Objects   (for early childhood)
                  and
Crystals, Insects and Unknown Objects   (intermediate level)
both by
McGavack and LaSalle
The John Day Company
257 Park Avenue South
New York, N. Y.   10010

Discovering the Outdoors
by
Laurence Pringle, Editor
The Natural History Press (publisher)
Garden City, New York

How To Do An Experiment
by
Philip Goldstein
Harcour Brace and Jovanovick, Inc. (publisher)

Content Areas (Miscellaneous):

Manual for Measurement Science
   Ohaus Scale Corporation
   1050 Commerce Avenue
   Union, New Jersey   07083

Handbook of Nature Study
by Anna Botsford Comstock
   Comstock Publishing Co.
   Ithaca, New York

The Earth Beneath Us   (Geology)
by Kirtley F. Mather
Random House
New York, N. Y.

The Scientist
by Henry Morgenau
   Time-Life Books, Inc.
   Life Science Library
   (also all other iddues in the Life
   Science and Nature Library)

Common Native Animals
by Vessel and Harrington
Chandler Publishing Company
Scranton, Pennsylvania

The Book of Wild Pets
by Clifford B. Moore
Charles T. Branford Co.
Boston, Massachusetts

Others:

Science and Survival by Barry Commoner; Viking Press

The Forest and the Sea by Marston Bates; Mentor Books

Our Wildlife Legacy by Durwood Allen; Funk and Wagnalls

The Web of Life and Man in the Web of Life by John Storer; Signet Science Library

Biology . . . Its People and Its Papers by Baumel and Berger; National
    Science Teachers Association.

SOURCES OF INFORMATION REGARDING THE ENVIRONMENT AND ENVIRONMENTAL EDUCATION

Organizations:

American Forestry Association
919 Seventeenth St. N. W.
Washington, D. C. 20006

American Petroleum Institute
1271 Avenue of the Americas
New York, N. Y. 10020

Animal Welfare Institute
P. O. Box 3492
Grand Central Station
New York, N. Y. 10017

Association for Voluntary Sterilization
14 West 40th Street
New York, N. Y. 10018

Bureau of Land Management
U. S. Department of the Interior
Washington, D. C. 20050

Common Cause
2100 M Street, N. W.
Washington, D. C. 20037

Conservation Foundation
1250 Connecticut Ave., N. W.
Washington, D. C. 20036

Division of Air Pollution
Public Health Service
U. S. Dept. of Health, Education and Welfare
Washington, D. C. 20201

Environmental Action, Inc.
Room 731
1346 Connecticut Avenue, N. W.
Washington, D. C. 20036

Environmental Defense Fund
P. O. Drawer 740
Stony Brook. New York 11790

Federal Water Pollution Control Admin.
Office of Public Information
Washington, D. C. 20242

Forest Service
U. S. Dept. of Agriculture
Washington, D. C. 20250

Friends of the Earth
30 East 42nd Street
New York, N. Y. 10017

Garden Club of America
Conservation Committee
598 Madison Avenue
New York, N. Y. 10022

Illinois Natural History Survey
Natural Resources Building
Urbana, Illinois 61801

Ill. State Dept. of Conservation
Springfield, Illinois 62706

Illinois State Geological Survey
Natural Resources Building
Urbana, Illinois 61801

Illinois State Museum
Spring and Edwards Street
Springfield, Illinois 62106

Izaak Walton League
1326 Waukegan Road
Glenview, Illinois 60025

John Muir Institute for
Environmental Studies
451 Pacific Avenue
San Francisco, California 94133

League of Conservation Voters
917 Fifteenth St., N. W.
Washington, D. C. 20005

Midwest Coal Producers Institute
Wildwood Lane
Springfield, Illinois 62700

National Air Pollution Control
Administration
Federal Building
26 Federal Plaza
New York, N. Y. 10007

National Audubon Society
1130 Fifth Avenue
New York, N. Y. 10028

National Wildlife Federation
1412 Sixteenth St., N. W.
Washington, D. C. 20036

The Nature Conservancy
1522 K Street, N. W.
Washington, D. C. 20005

Planned Parenthood-World
Population
515 Madison Avenue
New York, N. Y. 10022

Population Crisis Committee
1730 K Street, N. W.
Washington, D. C. 20006

Population Reference Bureau
1755 Massachusetts Ave., N. W.
Washington, D. C. 20036

Resources for the Future, Inc.
1145 19th Street, N. W.
Washington, D. C. 20005

Sierra Club
1050 Mills Tower
San Francisco, California 94104

Soil Conservation Service
U. S. Dept. of Agriculture
Washington, D. C. 20401

Superintendent of Documents
Government Printing Office
Washington, D. C. 20402

The Wilderness Society
729 Fifteenth St., N. W.
Washington, D. C. 20005

Zero Population Growth
367 State Street
Los Altos, California 94022

Teaching Aids:

Environmental Education Instruction Plans
available from
  Conservation and Environmental Education Center
  5400 Glenwood Avenue
  Minneopolis, Minnesota 55422

Environmental Education - Objectives and Field Activities
available from
  Paducah Public Schools
  Environmental Education
  10th and Clark Streets
  P. O. Box 1137
  Paducah, Kentucky 42001

Guidelines for Environmental Sensitivity
available from
  Pennsylvania Department of Education
  Commonwealth of Pennsylvania
  Harrisburg, Pennsylvania 17126

Man and His Environment: An Introduction to Using Environmental Study Areas
available from
  Association of Classroom Teachers
  National Education Association
  1201 Sixteenth Street, N. W.
  Washington, D. C. 20036

People and Their Environment: Teachers' Curriculum Guides to Conservation
Education (Matthew Brennan, Editor)
available from
  J. G. Ferguson Publishing Co.
  6 North Michigan Avenue
  Chicago, Illinois 60602

Teachers Guide for Environmental Education
available from
  The Task Force on Environment and Natural Resources
  The North Carolina Dept. of Public Instruction
  Raleigh, North Carolina

Synopsis of Games and Simulations in ERCA Life Science by Fred Rasmussen
available from
  Educational Research Council of America
  Rockerfeller Building
  Cleveland, Ohio 44113

Ecosources Bibliography*
available from
  Ms. Janet Woerner
  Freeland Community Schools
  Freeland, Michigan 48623
* send stamped, self-addressed envelopes in order to receive this free monthly
publication.

A <u>Selected</u> <u>List</u> <u>of</u> <u>Urban</u> <u>and</u> <u>Environmental</u> <u>Gaming</u>/<u>Simulations</u>
available from
    The University of Michigan
    Extension Gaming Service
    412 Maynard Street
    Ann Arbor, Michigan 48104

<u>Ecologos</u> <u>Spring</u> <u>1972</u> (bibliography)
available from
    Sidney Kramer Books
    1722 H Street, N. W.
    Washington, D. C. 20006

<u>Environmental</u> <u>Education</u> <u>in</u> <u>the</u> <u>Elementary</u> <u>School</u> (by Sale and Lee)
available from
    Holt Rinehart and Winston

<u>Field</u> <u>Book</u> <u>of</u> <u>Nature</u> <u>Activities</u> <u>and</u> <u>Conservation</u> (by William Hullcourt)
available from
    G. P. Putnam's Sons
    200 Madison Avenue
    New York, N. Y. 10016

<u>Techniques</u> <u>for</u> <u>Teaching</u> <u>Conservation</u> Education (by Brown and Mauser)
<u>Conservation</u> <u>for</u> <u>Camp</u> <u>and</u> <u>Classroom</u> (by Robert O. Bale)
both available from
    Burgess Publishing Company
    426 S. Sixth Street
    Minneapolis, Minnesota 55415

<u>Process</u> <u>Modules</u> <u>for</u> <u>Investigating</u> <u>Environmental</u> <u>Science</u> (by Hungerford and
Litherland)
available from
    Mr. Ralph Litherland
    Special Services
    Carbondale.School District
    606 W. Pecan
    Carbondale, Illinois 62901

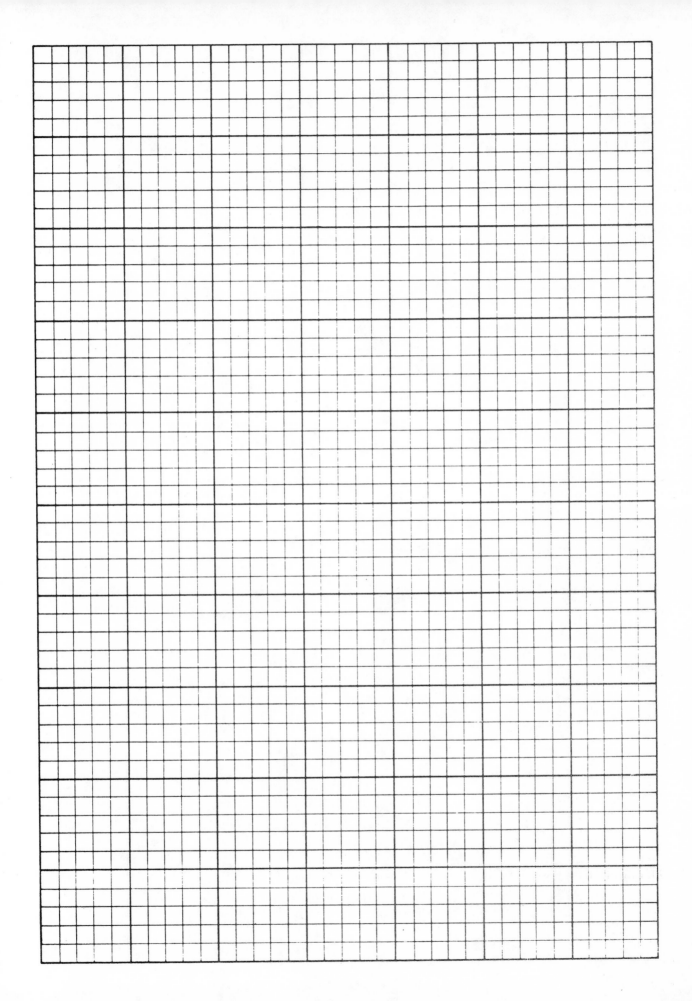

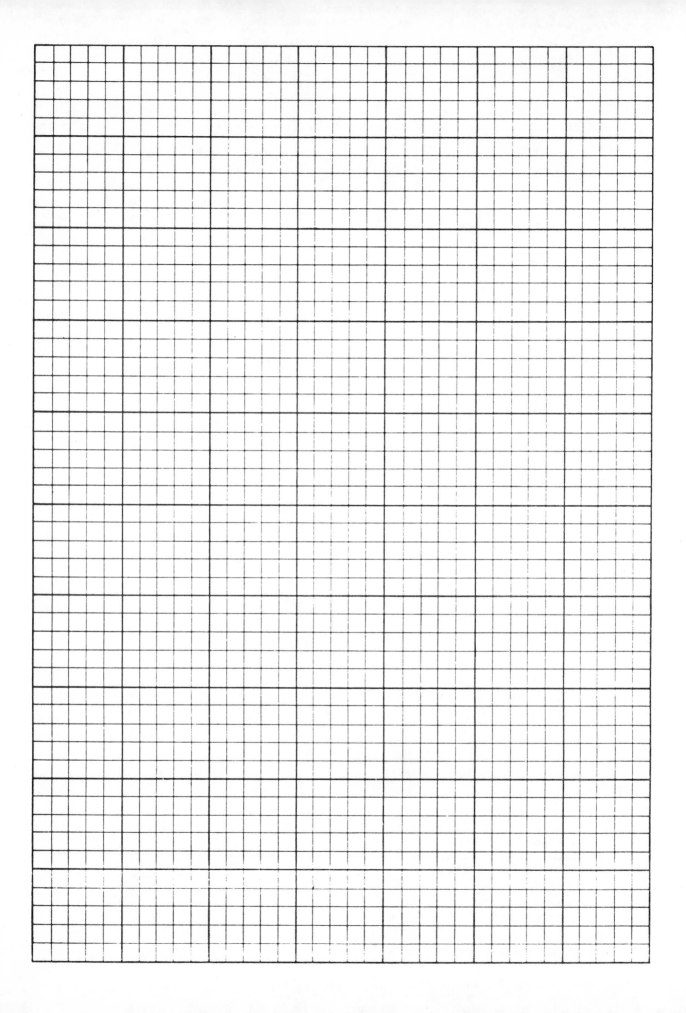

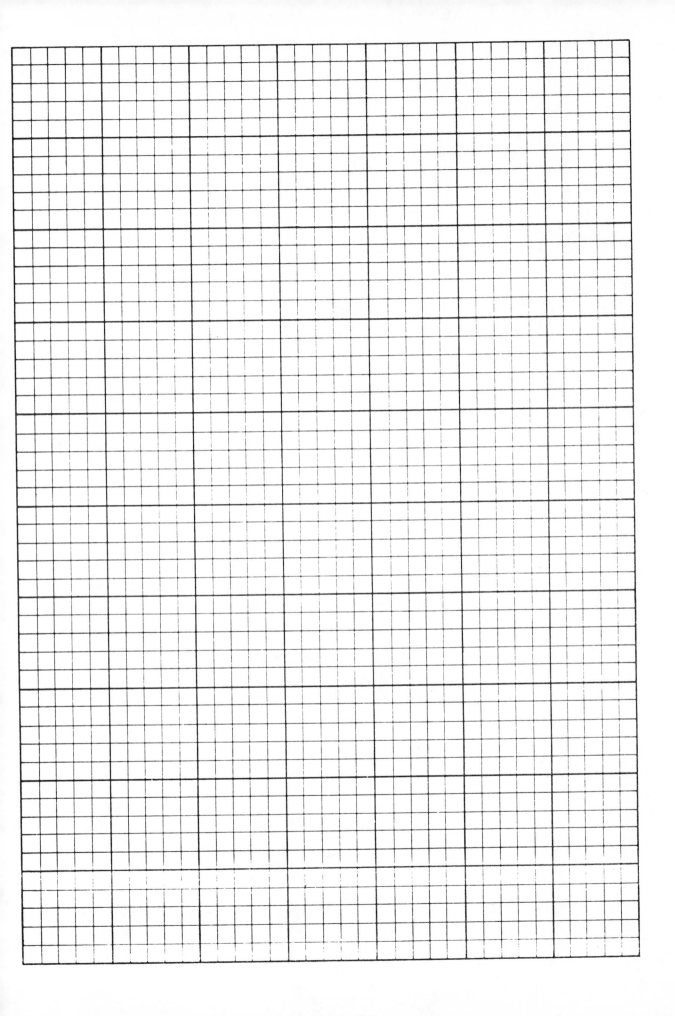